Dribble Drabble

# Dribble Drabble

## PROCESS ART EXPERIENCES for YOUNG CHILDREN

### DEYA BRASHEARS HILL

**Redleaf Press®**
www.redleafpress.org
800-423-8309

Published by Redleaf Press
10 Yorkton Court
St. Paul, MN 55117
www.redleafpress.org

The activities in this book were previously self-published under the titles *Dribble Drabble* and *More Dribble Drabble*

First edition 2016
Cover design by Jim Handrigan
Cover illustration by Ian Handrigan
Interior design by Douglas Schmitz
Typeset in Utopia and Sketchnote Square
Printed in the United States of America

Library of Congress Cataloging-in-Publication Data
Names: Hill, Deya Brashears, author.
Title: Dribble drabble : process art experiences for young children / Deya Brashears Hill.
Description: First edition. | St. Paul, MN : Redleaf Press, 2016.
Identifiers: LCCN 2016003921 (print) | LCCN 2016005276 (ebook) | ISBN 9781605545288 (pbk.) | ISBN 9781605545295 (ebook)
Subjects: LCSH: Art--Technique. | Creative activities and seat work.
Classification: LCC N7440 .H45 2016 (print) | LCC N7440 (ebook) | DDC 701/.8--dc23
LC record available at http://lccn.loc.gov/2016003921

Printed on acid-free paper                                                        U20-03

# Contents

INTRODUCTION . . . . . . . . . . . . . . . . . . 1

SUPPLIES . . . . . . . . . . . . . . . 9

PART 1:   PAINTING. . . . . . . . . . . . . .11

PART 2:   CRAYONS. . . . . . . . . . . . . 31

PART 3:   COLLAGE AND SCULPTURE . . . 41

PART 4:   MODELING MATERIALS . . . . . 59

PART 5:   CHALK . . . . . . . . . . . . . . 77

PART 6:   PRINTING . . . . . . . . . . . . 85

PART 7:   JUST FOR FUN . . . . . . . . . . 99

GLOSSARY OF ART MATERIAL TERMS . . .106

# Introduction

Early childhood teachers know that offering art experiences for young children is of vital importance. Creative art should offer children the opportunity for originality, creativity, fluency, flexibility, sensitivity, and aesthetics. Art is one discipline where no one way of doing things is right or wrong. Children are unique in their artistic expression. As teachers, we must remember the goal when providing appropriate art experiences is the process of creating art and not the finished product.

*Dribble Drabble* is a collection of hands-on, process-oriented art activities that have been used successfully in the classroom and at home. The art experiences presented in this book are written primarily for preschool children but are easily modified for infants and toddlers as well as school-age children. The activities are also easy to prepare, set up, and adapt to a project-approach curriculum. They provide the opportunity for young children's success and—most importantly—for fun.

## Stages of Artistic Development

All children pass through a sequential pattern of artistic development. Some go through the various stages quickly; others may take their time; and all go back and repeat the earlier stages as they progress through their development.

There are various stages of artistic development ranging from the scribble stage to recognizable art. Let's take a closer look at the generally accepted stages of artistic development. Keep in mind that the indicated ages are simply generalizations and not rigid guidelines for all children. Also notice that the ages overlap throughout the stages of art development.

**Scribble Stage** Ages 2–3. The creation of scribbles is the basis for all young children's art. Children begin by using various art media to scribble and eventually form scribbles involving vertical, horizontal, diagonal, curving, and circular lines.

**Single Shapes** Ages 2–4. Once the scribble stage is mastered, circles, crosses, squares, rectangles, and other basic shapes become roughly visible in young children's art. In this stage, children do not yet have the motor ability to master more complex shapes.

**Combined Shapes** Ages 3–5. Children create designs by combining and repeating various shapes. Placing shapes within shapes is common.

**Mandalas and Suns** Ages 3–5. Images of mandalas and suns are common in young children's art, symbols that can be traced back to prehistoric times. When children begin to create these images, it is a turning point in their artistic development. From this stage, we begin to see the emergence of more recognizable art.

**People** Ages 4–5. When young children first begin drawing people, the images appear as a large head with arms and legs extending from the head. As children continue their artistic development, a trunk and more details appear in their drawing.

**Beginning Recognizable Art** Ages 4–6. At this stage, children's pictures are mostly identifiable. Young children create art using the figures and shapes mastered during previous stages of artistic development. Their artwork may still contain several unrelated objects.

**Later Recognizable Art** Ages 5–7. The entire piece of art tells a story. You may see birds, trees, people, flowers, suns, houses, and kites. Children in this stage may still prefer to draw abstract art; however, this is done with good control and intent.

# Creating a Stimulating Art Environment

Teachers, caregivers, and parents often ask what they should provide for their children in order to give them a quality art experience. There are four basic areas that should be a part of every early childhood art environment: easels, a free art table, a tactile or sensory experience, and an activity center. Children should be able to choose from at least two of these areas each day, and in an ideal setting, all four areas can be used. Let's take a look at each item in detail and its artistic value.

## EASELS

The easel is an art experience that many teachers and parents would prefer to do without; easels take up space, and mixing and cleaning paints can get routine. However, incredible value can be gained from this form of expression that cannot be derived from any other art medium. The fine muscles in the fingers and toes are last to develop in young children, and easels provide the perfect vertical experience to aid this development.

From the beginning of time, children all over the world have drawn on the walls. This tells us that the natural means of artistic expression for young children is in the vertical plane. Creating art on a vertical plane is possible with the use of the easel. For this reason, it is vital that as teachers we take the time to provide opportunities for quality easel exploration.

Here are some suggestions for using easels:

- Purchasing an expensive easel is not necessary. Tape paper to a wall, door, or a smooth fence outside.

- If you purchase an easel, consider getting one that attaches to the wall. This will conserve floor space. Classrooms should have at least two vertical surfaces for every ten children.

- Don't use only rectangular paper. Have children cut paper into other shapes, or cut shapes from the paper and use the paper that remains (negative space).

- Use quality easel paper rather than copy paper or thin newsprint.

- Use quality paint in clear, bright colors.

- Use alternate materials as paintbrushes. Try using feathers, cotton swabs, sponges, flowers, pine branches, or whatever seems interesting to the children.

- Add salt or glitter to the paint for a different effect and texture.
- Try chalk sometimes instead of paint. Tape four different colors of chalk together with masking tape. When a child draws on the paper, many different colors will emerge.
- Offer the easel experience both indoors and outside.

### Role of the Teacher in the Easel Area

Prior to inviting children into the easel area, the teacher must take time each day to ensure that the space is prepared. Brushes and other painting utensils should be in good condition and include both short- and long-handled brushes. The paints should be mixed well and paint tubs filled. Quality easel paper should be plentiful and easily available.

Once children are ready to begin, the teacher or caregiver should encourage children to first put their names on their artwork. Even young children can attempt to write their names. If adult assistance is necessary, the teacher should ask permission to put the artist's name on the artwork and where the child's name should go. This shows respect for both the child and his work.

During the art exploration, the teacher or caregiver may want to take the opportunity to encourage children's language development by asking questions such as "Would you like to tell me about your picture?" Sometimes the child will have a long story, and sometimes she will not want to say anything. Do not ask the child yes or no questions such as "Is that a bird?" This type of closed questioning does not encourage language development and can intimidate a child into feeling that their artwork "should" look like something specific. The easel experience should always be inviting and focus on the process of creating art as opposed to the finished product.

Once the artwork is finished, the child should hang it to dry; the teacher may need to help with this. New paper should then be placed on the easel for the next child to use.

## FREE ART TABLE

In this area, art supplies can be set out for the children to use at will. The table should have a variety of the following materials:

- clear tape (in a bottom-weighted tape dispenser)
- crayons
- envelopes
- felt-tip pens

- hole punches
- markers
- paper in various sizes, shapes, colors, and textures
- pencils (colored pencils)
- scissors
- stamps
- staplers
- sticky dots
- other tools that might lend themselves to creative expression

The free art table should be free of any models of artwork or "color-in" types of activities. It's amazing what young children can create with unrestricted options.

### Role of the Teacher at the Free Art Table

In this area, the teacher's or caregiver's primary role is to keep supplies furnished, make sure the children's names are on their artwork, and occasionally tidy the table. Young children love to make a mess while exploring art, but they do not like to sit down to one. Prepare the art table each day by keeping supplies plentiful, in good working order, and attractive. Children's interest is piqued and they become involved when the art supplies are out and available at the table, enticing them to create.

## TACTILE, OR SENSORY, AREA

People of all ages enjoy tactile, or sensory, expression, and this kind of experience should be available to young children as often as possible. These experiences best take place in a sensory table or bucket. Clean kitty litter pans make excellent sensory bins because they offer a flat bottom and ample size for exploration. Some items that work well for sensory exploration with young children include sand, mud, cornmeal, warm water, large pieces of potpourri, "goop" (cornstarch and water), hay, birdseed, or whatever you feel offers a great sensory experience and interests the children. When choosing items for sensory play, keep in mind children's allergies as well as choking hazards. It is important to keep tactile play safe and fun!

Providers often forget about good old water play. This is still one of the most soothing experiences we can provide for young children. Occasionally, you can color the water using liquid watercolors and add some bubbles using liquid soap. Sponges, pumps, hoses, and various containers can also add to the fun of water play. Sand (indoors, rather than just in the outdoor sandbox) and mud also provide many options for sensory experiences. Other possibilities for tactile materials include modeling materials such as clay, playdough, and sand clay.

### Role of the Teacher in the Tactile, or Sensory, Area

Prior to children exploring sensory materials, teachers should try the sensory experience for themselves. Explore the sensory area through the eyes of a child in your classroom. If you have included modeling mediums in the area, is the clay too hard or too dry? Is the water too cold? The teacher or caregiver should occasionally sweep or mop the surrounding area to keep it safe and inviting for the children.

## ACTIVITY CENTER

An activity center is an area in the classroom where children are able to use the established materials to engage in art exploration. This area needs adult support in order to make it work in the classroom. Teachers, of course, do not do the work for the children nor do they make a model for the children to copy; however, adults are necessary to support the activity flow and supervise the children.

In the activity center, supplies must be replenished, and some common guidelines or ground rules should be offered to the children. Variations in the activities that are discovered by the children are encouraged at all times. There is no "right way" to do the activities in this center. The various activities offered throughout this book fall into this category of process art and would be excellent choices for the activity center in your classroom.

### Role of the Teacher in the Activity Center

This area requires adult interaction. It is most successful when the provider sits down with the children and chats informally. The teacher may want to do some of the activities alongside the children while engaged in conversation. If adults create their own artwork, it is important that they are careful not to make a model for the children to copy or aspire to. Overall, teachers should keep the activity center available and simple; put children's names on the activities, and keep the area tidy and inviting.

# A Word about Cost

Most early learning programs have limited or tight budgets to work with. Program directors and teachers are always looking for ways to save money. There are ways to conserve funds in some areas of the art environment, while in others quality materials are a must.

For example, in the center where I was a director for fourteen years, I saved a great deal of money on paper supplies. Instead of using construction paper or poster board (both of which can be expensive), I was able to get matte board for free from a local framing shop. The frame shop staff were delighted that we were able to repurpose the matte board scraps in our classroom so they would not have to throw it away. These scraps would often come in various shapes and sizes, and sometimes I would cut them into a specific size for a planned activity. I also used matte board for almost everything at the activity table—collage, painting, crayons, chalk, and sculpture.

Another cost-saving option is to have paper supplies donated. For example, banks gave me envelopes and deposit slips (the children had a ball with those). Pharmacies gave me tablets of paper that they had received with various medications. These were often unusual shapes and colors, which the children enjoyed. Printing shops and newspaper companies would donate the ends of paper rolls. Some greeting card stores would even save envelopes after holidays; they had to send the cards back to the company but often threw away the bright, cheerfully colored envelopes.

While I saved a lot of money on those paper supplies, I found that certain areas within the art environment demanded more expensive tools. Young children do not use the easel nearly as much when copy paper or newsprint is attached as they do when nice white easel or butcher paper is available. Paints should be bright and attractive rather than muted and dull. Quality staplers, scissors, and tape dispensers are also a must. Crayons and felt-tip pens should be high quality and should be replaced often—pens that are running out of ink are difficult and frustrating to use.

Using real clay rather than plasticine clay provides a much more pliable and creative clay experience for young children. Fresh playdough and goop will keep children occupied for hours, but dried-out materials will disinterest them immediately. White school glue is necessary so that children do not get frustrated with the gluing experience. Paste and glue can provide very different experiences. Using both may offer variety for the children; however, paste can be somewhat frustrating for young children.

A quality art environment demands quality materials that work well. It takes time, patience, and energy to find the appropriate supplies, and it takes price comparison to get the best quality for your program's budget. The children in your care will truly have a positive art experience if you take the time to make their exploration the top priority.

## Final Thoughts

In summary, if your program has minimal staff, offering the easel and the free art area each day will provide a creative, fun, and exciting art experience for all children, without the need for extensive adult supervision. The other two areas—tactile, or sensory, and activity centers—should be offered as often as possible with the direct support of a teacher or caregiver. As you plan for art experiences in your classroom, remember the following:

- Vary the choice of available materials and move items around the art space to create an appealing display.
- Offer all four art areas both inside and outside.
- Vary the types and colors of paper available to children.
- Softly play background music or display prints of fine art to inspire young artists.

When an adult sits down with children to experience art alongside them, the children are much more likely to become involved for longer periods of time. Simply sitting down at their level offers your companionship and support. It makes each child feel special. Many enlightening conversations have evolved while I enjoyed an art experience with young children. If you have fun, they will too.

# Supplies

Here is a list of supplies that you may want to collect for your classroom art environment.

Aluminum foil

Bangles

Berry baskets

Bleach mixture for cleanup (keep out of reach of children)

Bowls and other containers (various sizes)

Bows or ribbon

Boxes (various sizes and shapes)

Brayers (or small rollers)

Butcher paper

Cardboard

Cellophane

Chalk (colored and white)

Clear tape

Coffee filters

Collage items

Combs

Confetti

Construction paper (all colors)

Contact paper (clear)

Cookie cutters

Cookie sheets

Corks

Cornstarch

Cotton balls

Cotton swabs

Craft sticks

Crayons

Driftwood

Egg cartons

Electric iron (keep out of reach of children)

Epsom salts

Eyedroppers

Fabric pieces

Feathers

Felt-tip pens

Flower petals (dried)

Funnels (small and large)

Glitter

Glue brushes

Grass (dried)

Hole punches

Ice cube trays

Lace

Leaves

Lids (various sizes)

Liquid tempera paint

Liquid watercoloring (food coloring

Marbles

Masking tape

Matte board

Measuring cups and spoons
Muffin tins
Newspaper
Oil pastels
Paintbrushes
Paper (all kinds)
Paper plates
Pencil sharpener
Pencils (colored)
Pie tins or cake pans
Pitchers
Plastic bags (various sizes)
Plaster of paris
Poster board
Pot holders
Potato mashers
Powdered tempera paint
Rags
Rock salt
Rocks
Rubber bands
Rubber cement (keep out of reach of children)
Rubber gloves
Rubbing alcohol (keep out of reach of children)
Salad spinner
Salt
Saltshakers
Sand
Sand sifters
Sandpaper (various grades)

Sawdust
Scissors
Shaker bottles
Shaving cream
Shells
Sponges
Spoons
Spray bottles
Squeeze bottles
Stamp pads
Stamps
Stencils
Straws
Strings
Styrofoam (various sizes)
Tape dispenser
Tissue paper
Toilet tissue tubes
Tongs
Toothpicks
Towels (cloth and paper)
Trays
Velvet
Watercolor paint
Waxed paper
White paper
White school glue
Wire mesh screening
Wood
Wrapping paper
Yarn

# PART 1

# Painting

# Cotton Ball Art

**MATERIALS NEEDED:**
White paper
Powdered tempera paint
Small bowls filled with water
Paintbrushes of various sizes
Cotton balls

**PROCEDURE:**
- Give each child a piece of paper.
- Allow the children to use cotton balls to draw or dab on the paper with powdered tempera paint.
- After completing the powdered tempera drawing, let each child use a paintbrush to paint the entire paper with water. See what happens to the dry paint!
- Allow the children to experiment with this medium. Colors will combine and change right before their eyes.

# Anything Can Be a Paintbrush

**MATERIALS NEEDED:**
White paper
Liquid tempera paint
Bowls
Cotton swabs
Eye makeup brushes
Feathers
Cotton balls

**PROCEDURE:**
- Give each child a piece of paper.
- Place small amounts of liquid tempera into bowls.
- Allow each child to select a tool (cotton swab, brush, feather, or cotton ball) and paints. Have the children dip their tools into the paint and draw on the paper to create unique paintings.

# Tree Branch Painting

**MATERIALS NEEDED:**
White paper
Liquid tempera paint
Cookie sheets or other wide, flat containers
Pine tree branches

**PROCEDURE:**
- Give each child a piece of paper.
- Pour liquid tempera paint onto cookie sheets.
- Allow the children to dip pine tree branches into the paint.
- Have the children slap the paint-covered branches onto the paper.
- See how many designs the children can make with the branches and their brushstrokes.

# Ink Blots

**MATERIALS NEEDED:**
White paper
Liquid tempera paint
Water
Bowls
Eyedroppers

**PROCEDURE:**
- Have the children fold each piece of paper in half along either the length or width.
- Pour liquid tempera paint into two or three small bowls.
- Add a small amount of water to each bowl to thin the paint.
- Have the children open their folded piece of paper and lay it flat on the table.
- Allow the children to use eyedroppers to squirt paint onto the paper.
- Have the children fold the paper along the crease and press the sides together.
- Open and see the symmetrical design.

# Squeegee Paint Pull

**MATERIALS NEEDED:**
Large sheet of white, nonporous paper
Liquid tempera paint
Window squeegees
Tape

**PROCEDURE:**
- Cover a table with the paper, and tape the edges to the table.
- Drip several colors of paint along each edge of the paper.
- Have the children pull the various colors of paint across the paper with window squeegees. See how the different colors blend.

# Shiny Art Painting

**MATERIALS NEEDED:**
Matte board, cardboard, or other sturdy material
Liquid dishwashing or hand soap
Corn syrup
Liquid tempera paint or liquid watercolors
Small bowls
Paintbrushes
Mixing spoons
Measuring spoons

**MIXTURE (PER CHILD):**
1½ teaspoons dishwashing or hand soap
4 tablespoons corn syrup
Liquid tempera or liquid watercolors

Mix ingredients until well blended. Repeat to make several colors. Pour into small bowls.

**PROCEDURE:**
- Give each child a matte board, cardboard, or other base material.
- Have the children paint designs on their base material.

# Sparkle Sprinkle

**MATERIALS NEEDED:**
Matte board, paper plates, or poster board
Liquid tempera paint
White school glue
Glitter
Bowls
Spoons

**PROCEDURE:**
- In separate bowls, combine equal parts of white school glue and one color of tempera paint.
- Give each child a piece of matte board or poster board, or a paper plate.
- Allow the children to spoon the paint mixtures onto their boards.
- Have the children twist and turn the boards to see the paint run and make designs.
- Sprinkle glitter over wet glue mixture.

# Liquid Watercolors Paper Towels

**MATERIALS NEEDED:**
Coffee filters, paper towels, or white tissue paper
Liquid watercolors
Water
Bowls
Eyedroppers

**PROCEDURE:**
- Mix up three or four colors of liquid watercolors and water in separate bowls.
- Give each child a paper towel, coffee filter, or piece of white tissue paper.
- Have the children use eyedroppers to squirt liquid watercolor mixture onto their paper. Colors will run together and change.
- This activity makes great wrapping paper once it is dry.

# Speckled Tissue

**MATERIALS NEEDED:**
Tissue paper
Liquid bleach diluted in water
Cotton swabs
Smocks or aprons

**PROCEDURE:**
- Let each child select a sheet of tissue paper.
- Give each child a smock or apron.
- Allow the children to dip their cotton swabs into the bleach mixture and paint it onto the tissue paper.
- This process will take the color out of the paper and give a streaked effect.

Note: Be careful to supervise children with the bleach. Smocks or aprons should be worn at all times, and no more than four children should do this activity at once.

# Marble–Golf Ball Roll Painting

**MATERIALS NEEDED:**
White paper
Liquid tempera paint
Large, shallow box (Kitty litter pan works well.)
5 or 6 marbles and/or 2 golf balls
Salt (optional)

**PROCEDURE:**
- Cut paper to fit the shallow box and place it into the bottom of the box.
- Have the children scoop one spoonful of each color of liquid tempera paint onto the paper.
- Place the marbles and/or golf balls in the box.
- Allow the children to roll the marbles around in the paint by gently shaking the box.
- The marbles will cause the paint to streak across the paper and create designs.

Optional: Add a small amount of salt to the paint. It will crystallize as it dries.

# Bubble Blowing Painting

**MATERIALS NEEDED:**
Trays, paper plates, or white paper
4 small containers
Liquid watercolors
Bubble solution and bubble wands

**PROCEDURE:**
- Fill each of the four containers with bubble solution.
- Add one color of liquid watercolors (green, yellow, red, blue) to each container. Letting the liquid watercolor mixtures stand overnight works best.
- Once ready to use the mixture, place a bubble wand in each container.
- Give each child a tray, paper plate, or sheet of white paper.
- Have the children dip wands into the solution and blow bubbles either onto the tray, paper plate, or white paper.
- If children blow colored bubbles on a tray, have a piece of paper ready for them to press down over blown bubbles to capture the imprint.

# Twist Painting

**MATERIALS NEEDED:**
Heavy paper
Liquid tempera paint
Squeeze bottles

**PROCEDURE:**
- Have the children stand near a table and squeeze three or four dots of liquid tempera paint directly onto the tabletop. Paint drops can range from pea size to dime size.
- Guide the children to place paper on top of the paint drops and twist the paper with the heels of their hands about one-half turn.
- Have the children lift their papers and see their designs.

# Shaker Painting

**MATERIALS NEEDED:**
Heavy paper or poster board
Powdered tempera paint
Salt
White school glue thinned with water
Bowls
Shaker bottles
Glue brushes

**PROCEDURE:**
- Fill each shaker bottle with a mixture of half salt and half tempera paint.
- Pour watered-down glue into bowls.
- Give each child a piece of paper or poster board. The paper or poster board can be cut into shapes or left whole.
- Let the children use glue brushes to paint the glue onto their paper.
- Have the children sprinkle the salt and paint mixture onto the glue.
- When the paint and glue mixtures combine, they create a knobby effect.

# Foot Painting and Prints

**MATERIALS NEEDED:**
Large sheet of paper
Liquid tempera paint
Paintbrushes
Chair
Soapy water

**PROCEDURE:**
- Place a large sheet of paper on the ground.
- Have each child sit in the chair while you use a paintbrush to paint the bottom of his feet.
- Allow the children to walk on the paper or to make designs with their toes.
- Children should sit and soak feet in soapy water to get them clean and wipe dry with towels.

# Spot Design Painting

**MATERIALS NEEDED:**
White construction paper
Watercolor paint
Water
Sponges
Paintbrushes

**PROCEDURE:**
- Give each child a sheet of paper.
- Guide the children to sponge water on both sides of the construction paper.
- Have the children load their paintbrushes with watercolor paint and drip or flick color onto the paper.
- Allow them to repeat this process using various colors and watch the colors blend together.

# Spray Bottle Painting

**MATERIALS NEEDED:**
White construction paper
Liquid tempera paint
Paintbrushes
Spray bottle filled with water
White school glue thinned with water (optional)
Glitter (optional)

**PROCEDURE:**
- Give each child a sheet of paper.
- Have the children dip their paintbrushes into a desired color of paint, then hold their brushes over the paper, allowing the paint to drip onto the paper.
- Children can then spray the paint drops with water and watch paint streams form on the paper.

Optional: After the paint dries, children may want to drip glue onto the paper and sprinkle glitter.

# Dangle and Swing Painting

**MATERIALS NEEDED:**
Butcher paper
Liquid tempera paint
Paintbrushes of various sizes
String
Clear tape

**PROCEDURE:**
- Tape a large piece of butcher paper onto the floor.
- Tie strings around the handles of the paintbrushes.
- Let the children dip the brushes into paint.
- Have each child stand and hold the brush by the string, letting the brush dangle and swing onto the paper.

# Watercolors—a Different Approach

**MATERIALS NEEDED:**
White paper
Watercolor paint
Bowls
Water
Sponges
Paintbrushes

**PROCEDURE:**
- Give each child a sheet of white paper.
- Have the children use the sponges to wet the entire paper with water.
- Let the children use paintbrushes to paint freely with the watercolors on the wet paper.
- Help the children learn how to clean the brushes between colors and how to use the water with the paints.

# Black Line Design

**MATERIALS NEEDED:**
White construction paper
Black liquid tempera paint
Bright-colored liquid tempera paint
Paintbrushes

**PROCEDURE:**

- Give each child a sheet of white construction paper.
- Ask the children to paint lines using black liquid tempera paint. Encourage them to start from the middle of the paper and make the lines go off the edge.
- Let the pictures dry.
- Have the children paint inside the black lines with bright, shiny colors.

# Mud Painting

**MATERIALS NEEDED:**
Matte board, cardboard, or other sturdy base
Powdered tempera paint
Dirt
Water
Bowls (large and small)
Jumbo craft sticks
Paintbrushes of various types
Sand sifter

**PROCEDURE:**

- Have the children use the sand sifter to sift the dirt into a large bowl, and then separate the dirt into several small bowls.
- Add a small amount of powdered tempera paint to each bowl of dirt along with a small amount of water, and mix well.
- Let the children experiment freely with this medium. They can use paintbrushes, sponge brushes, or craft sticks to paint the mud paint on matte board, cardboard, or other base. Some children may want to use the mud as fingerpaint.
- If piled up, the mud may lend itself to a sculpture rather than a painting.

Note: Some children may choose to keep the natural mud color rather than adding tempera.

# Tissue Paper Paint

**MATERIALS NEEDED:**
White paper
Tissue paper
Several clear bowls of water
Paintbrushes

**PROCEDURE:**
- Have the children tear the tissue paper into small pieces.
- Then have each child place the torn tissue paper in the bowls of water and stir with the paintbrushes.
- After the water is colored, remove and discard the tissue paper and use the colored water for paint.
- Give each child a sheet of white paper.
- Allow the children to paint freely on the paper

# Fun with Watercolors

**MATERIALS NEEDED:**
Large sheet of thick paper
Watercolor paint
Water
Rubbing alcohol
Rock salt
Paintbrushes of various types
Eyedroppers
Masking tape

**PROCEDURE:**
- Tape the edges of the paper to the table.
- Have the children use paintbrushes to cover the paper with water.
- Let the children paint with watercolors on the paper.
- Next, have the children use eyedroppers to immediately drip rubbing alcohol onto their painting, and then have them sprinkle the rock salt on top of their painting.
- When paint is completely dry, wipe off the excess salt.

Note: Supervise the children closely when using rubbing alcohol.

# Homemade Paint

**MATERIALS NEEDED:**
Vinegar
Cornstarch
Liquid watercolors
Small container with a lid
Measuring spoons

### MIXTURE (PER CHILD):
½ teaspoon vinegar
½ teaspoon cornstarch
10 drops liquid watercolors

Put vinegar, cornstarch, and liquid watercolors into container. Cover and shake. If mixture is too thick, add vinegar. If too thin, add cornstarch.

**PROCEDURE:**
• Use as you would liquid tempera paint.

# Spinning Pictures

**MATERIALS NEEDED:**
White paper
Liquid tempera paint
Salad spinner
Spoons
Glitter (optional)

**PROCEDURE:**
• Cut paper to fit into the bottom of the salad spinner. Place paper in the spinner.
• Have the children use a spoon to drip paint onto the paper.
• Place the lid on the salad spinner and spin it. This requires some degree of coordination, and some younger children may need help.

Optional: Have the children sprinkle glitter on the paint before it dries.

# See-Through Murals

**MATERIALS NEEDED:**
Large sheets of colored cellophane
Liquid tempera paint
Bowls
Paintbrushes
Masking tape

**PROCEDURE:**
- Tape large sheets of cellophane to the window.
- Allow the children to paint with liquid tempera on the cellophane.
- Children will be able to see their translucent designs.

# Pendulum Painting

**MATERIALS NEEDED:**
Large sheet of paper
Powdered tempera paint
Liquid starch
Small, soft plastic funnel
Small pitcher
Strong string
Scissors

**PROCEDURE:**
- Tie a string around the lip at the large end of the funnel.
- Cut three pieces of string to 15 inches lengths and tie them equally spaced to the string that is around the lip.
- Tie the three loose ends of the string together, approximately 12 inches from the top of the funnel.
- Mix liquid starch and powdered tempera paint in pitcher. The paint should flow smoothly but not too fast.
- Place a large sheet of paper on the floor.
- Have each child hold the pendulum over the paper.
- Place the tip of your finger over the hole in the funnel while the child pours the paint in.
- Remove your finger and give the funnel a slight push.
- Have each child keep the pendulum movement going until all the paint has run out of the funnel.

# Tissue Paper Stain

**MATERIALS NEEDED:**

Matte board, cardboard, or other sturdy material
Tissue paper (3 or 4 different colors)
Bowls
Water
Paintbrushes
Spray bottles

**PROCEDURE:**

- Give each child a piece of matte board, cardboard, or other base material.
- Have children tear sheets of tissue paper into small pieces.
- Let children choose pieces—as many or as few as desired—and place them on their boards.
- Have the children paint water on top of the tissue pieces (spray bottles or paintbrushes can be used).
- Have them peel off the tissue paper and see the paint stain designs on their boards.

# Nuts and Bolts Painting

**MATERIALS NEEDED:**

White paper
Liquid tempera paint
Shallow box (large enough for paper to fit into)
Nuts and bolts of various sizes
Clear tape
Spoons

**PROCEDURE:**

- Cut the paper to fit into the box.
- Tape the paper to the bottom of the box.
- Let the children select some nuts and bolts to paint with. They may want to screw some of them together to create an interesting effect.
- Let each child spoon her choice of liquid tempera paint onto the paper.
- Children can now drop the nuts and bolts into the box and shake it, rolling them around in the paint to create unique designs.

# Paint the Snow

**MATERIALS NEEDED:**
Snow
Liquid watercolors or liquid tempera paint
Water
Bowls
Paintbrushes of various sizes
Powdered tempera paint (alternate)

**PROCEDURE:**
- Mix liquid watercolors and water, or use liquid tempera paint, and put into bowls.
- Take the children outside and let them use the paint or liquid watercolors to paint the snow.

Variation: Powdered tempera can be mixed with snow to create paint.

# Raindrop Painting

**MATERIALS NEEDED:**
White construction paper or other light-colored base material
Powdered tempera paint
Spray bottles filled with water
Saltshakers
Ice cubes (alternate)

**PROCEDURE:**
- Put powdered tempera paint into saltshakers.
- Let the children shake powdered tempera paint onto their white paper or other base.
- Encourage them to use several colors of powder.
- Have the children spray water onto the paper.
- The powdered tempera will turn into a painting once the water is added.

Variation: Instead of spraying their paintings with water, have the children run an ice cube over the dry paint and watch the colors appear.

Note: Powdered tempera paint can be dangerous if inhaled. Please use caution when using with young children.

# Felt-Tip Pen Spray Painting

**MATERIALS NEEDED:**
Paper towels, coffee filters, or other absorbent paper
Felt-tip pens of various colors
Spray bottles filled with water

**PROCEDURE:**
- Give each child a piece of absorbent paper.
- Have the children draw freely on the paper with felt-tip pens.
- Next, allow the children to spray water on their felt-tip pen drawings and see how the colors blend.

# Painting with Paste

**MATERIALS NEEDED:**
Matte board, cardboard, or other sturdy material
Liquid tempera paint
Paste
Bowls
Craft sticks
Mixing spoons
Measuring spoons
Beads, bangles, sticks, rocks, shells, and other small objects (optional)

**MIXTURE (PER CHILD):**
2 tablespoons liquid tempera paint
2 tablespoons paste

Mix together 2 tablespoons of each color of paint with 2 tablespoons paste in separate bowls.

**PROCEDURE:**
- Have the children use craft sticks to paint the paint mixture onto their matte board or cardboard.
- The mixture of paste and paint will create a textured effect.

Optional: Beads, bangles, sticks, rocks, shells, and other small objects can be added to the painting for a different textured effect.

# Homemade Watercolors

**MATERIALS NEEDED:**
Powdered or liquid tempera paint
Water
Small containers (ones used for sauces in fast-food restaurants work well)

**PROCEDURE:**
- Mix the powdered tempera paint with water, or use liquid tempera paint, and pour into the small containers.
- Let the paint dry for several days until it is hard.
- Once paint is hard, use as watercolor paint.

# Homemade Bubbles

**MATERIALS NEEDED:**
Powdered tempera paint
Water
Liquid starch
Liquid detergent
Container with lid for bubble mixture
Mixing spoons
Measuring cups

**MIXTURE:**
2 cups powdered tempera paint
1 cup water
½ cup liquid starch
1 cup liquid detergent

Stir powdered tempera paint and water together until smooth. (Liquid tempera can be used as a substitute for this mixture.) Add liquid starch and detergent and mix thoroughly. Add additional water if needed to create consistency of thin liquid soap.

**PROCEDURE:**
- Use bubble mixture as you would a store mixture.

# Tile Painting

**MATERIALS NEEDED:**
White ceramic tiles
Permanent felt-tip markers
Aprons

**PROCEDURE:**
- Give each child a tile and apron.
- Let the children draw freely on plain white tiles using permanent felt-tip markers.

Note: These markers will stain clothes, so an apron is advised.

# Salt Painting

**MATERIALS NEEDED:**
Matte board, cardboard, or paper plates
Liquid tempera paint or liquid watercolors
Liquid starch
Water
Salt
Bowls
Paintbrushes
Mixing spoons
Measuring cups and spoons

**MIXTURE (PER CHILD):**
$\frac{1}{8}$ cup liquid starch
$\frac{1}{8}$ cup water
1 teaspoon liquid tempera paint or 2 squirts of liquid watercolors
$\frac{1}{2}$ cup salt

Mix together liquid starch and water. Add paint or liquid watercolors.
Stir in salt. Mixture should be stirred continuously.

**PROCEDURE:**
- Give each child a matte board, cardboard, or paper plate.
- Let the children use paintbrushes to apply the mixture to their board or plate.

Note: Paint mixture will crystallize as it dries.

# Squeeze Painting

**MATERIALS NEEDED:**
Matte board or cardboard
Liquid tempera paint
Salt
Water
Flour
Bowls (large and small)
Squeeze bottles
Funnels
Mixing spoon
Measuring cups

**MIXTURE:**
2 cups salt
4–6 cups water
6 cups flour

Combine salt and water in large bowl, then stir in flour. Divide mixture into four small bowls, and stir a different color liquid tempera paint into each bowl. Using a funnel, pour mixture into squeeze bottles. It should run easily. Keep extra mixture ready to refill bottles.

**PROCEDURE:**
- Give each child a piece of matte board or cardboard.
- Allow each child to squeeze the paint mixture onto the board.
- Encourage the children to squeeze colors on top of the others and watch what happens.
- Let paintings dry.

# PART 2

# Crayons

# Crayon Rubbings

**MATERIALS NEEDED:**

White paper
Peeled crayons (Thicker crayons are best.)
Leaves, pine needles, shapes, sandpaper, coins, feathers, or other small objects

**PROCEDURE:**

- Give each child a sheet of white paper.
- Have various objects (such as leaves, sandpaper, feathers) available for the children to choose as a print.
- Let the children select some of the objects and put them under the paper.
- Have the children rub the paper with the side of the crayon, and the objects will show through as a print.

# Batik Design

**MATERIALS NEEDED:**

White paper
Crayons
Blue liquid tempera paint thinned with water
Paintbrushes

**PROCEDURE:**

- Give each child a piece of white paper.
- Allow the children to draw freely on the paper with crayons.
- Have them paint over their drawings with thinned paint.

# Watercolor Crayons

**MATERIALS NEEDED:**
White paper
Watercolor crayons, one set for each child
Water
Small bowls

**PROCEDURE:**
- Give each child a sheet of white paper, a set of watercolor crayons, and a small bowl of water.
- Have the children dip each crayon into the water and then draw with it. Watercolor crayons should not be left in water or they will melt.
- Children should empty their bowls of water and refill them with clean water as needed.

# Melted Crayons

**MATERIALS NEEDED:**
White paper or canvas
Peeled crayons
Hair dryer (for adult use only)
Double-sided tape

**PROCEDURE:**
- Give each child a piece of paper or canvas.
- Have the children use double-sided tape to stick crayons onto the paper or canvas.
- Use the hair dryer to melt the crayons adhered to the paper. This step should be completed only by an adult.
- It works best if crayons are melted downward. Start the heat from the top of the crayon and slowly work downward.
- Let the wax cool and dry, then use the dryer to melt the wax again. This creates multiple 3-D layers and designs.

# Wax Paper and Toilet Tissue Tube Kaleidoscope

**MATERIALS NEEDED:**
Waxed paper
Tissue paper
Toilet tissue tubes
Electric iron (for adult use only)
Rubber bands
Scissors
Peeled crayons (alternate)
Potato peeler (alternate) (for adult use only)

**PROCEDURE:**

- Cut waxed paper into rectangular pieces that when folded will amply fit over the end of the toilet tissue tube.
- Give each child a waxed paper square.
- Let the children cut or rip tiny pieces of tissue paper and place them on the waxed paper.

- Fold the waxed paper in half across the width and press with a warm iron until the paper sticks together. This should be done only by an adult.
- Assist the children in fastening the waxed paper to the end of the toilet tissue tube with a rubber band.
- Have them hold their tissue tubes up to the light to see the various colors.

Variation: Instead of using tissue paper, shred peeled crayons with a potato peeler (this should be done only by an adult), and have the children place the pieces on the waxed paper.

# Crayons and Watercolor

**MATERIALS NEEDED:**
White paper
Crayons
Watercolor paint
Paintbrushes

**PROCEDURE:**
- Give each child a sheet of paper.
- Have the children draw with crayons on the paper.
- Allow the children to use paintbrushes to paint with watercolors over the top of the crayon drawing.
- Watch the effect of crayons and watercolors run together.

# Crayon Swirls

**MATERIALS NEEDED:**
White paper
Peeled crayons

**PROCEDURE:**
- Give each child a piece of paper and a selection of peeled crayons.
- Have the children hold a crayon flat on its side and twist it in a circular motion to create crayon swirls on their paper.

# Melted Crayon Pictures

**MATERIALS NEEDED:**
Matte board, cardboard, felt, paper, balsa wood, or other sturdy material
Crayons of different sizes
Metal tray or baking sheet
Aluminum foil
Oven (for adult use only)
Rocks, shells, sticks, or other small objects (optional)

**PROCEDURE:**

- Cover the metal tray or baking sheet with aluminum foil.
- Place the matte board, cardboard, or other base material on the tray.
- Let the children place peeled crayons anywhere on the base material. Piled, stacked, or randomly placed is fine.
- Place the tray in a 250°F oven for about 10 minutes. This step should be completed only by an adult.
- Remove the tray and allow it to cool.

Optional: Offer rocks, shells, or other small objects to place in, around, and under the pile of crayons.

# Notched Crayons

**MATERIALS NEEDED:**
White paper
Peeled crayons
Table knife (for adult use only)

**PROCEDURE:**

- Use a table knife to cut notches into the edges of the peeled crayons. This step should be completed only by an adult.
- Give each child a piece of paper.
- Have the children rub a notched crayon on their paper. They will be able to see the effects of the thick and thin lines created by the notches in the crayon.

# Make Your Own Crayons

**MATERIALS NEEDED:**
White paper
Broken crayon bits
Hot plate (for adult use only)
Small pot with spout
Candy molds (Plastic molds work best.)

**PROCEDURE:**
- Let the children choose a selection of crayon bits.
- Melt the selected pieces on a hot plate over medium heat. This step should be completed only by an adult. Let the children watch this procedure. See new colors develop.
- Pour melted crayons into candy molds.
- Crayons harden quickly. Once they are cool, pop the crayons out of the molds.
- Allow the children to draw freely on a sheet of paper with their own crayons.

# See-Through Drawings

**MATERIALS NEEDED:**
White paper
Newspaper
Crayons
Baby oil or cooking oil
Cotton balls

**PROCEDURE:**
- Give each child a sheet of white paper, and then have the children place their white paper on top of a sheet of newspaper.
- Let the children draw freely with crayon on the white paper. Ask them to press hard.
- When the drawings are completed, have the children use a cotton ball to rub a small amount of oil over the back of the white paper.
- Place the oiled drawings back on the newspaper. Let these oil designs dry on newspaper.
- When the drawings are dry, have the children pick up their drawings and see how the oil has made them transparent.

# All-in-One Crayon

**MATERIALS NEEDED:**
White paper
Crayons
Masking tape

**PROCEDURE:**
- Have the children select three or four crayons of various colors.
- Use clear tape to tape the crayons together, creating one crayon. Make sure the points of the crayons are aligned.
- Children can use their all-in-one crayon to create designs and color on their paper.

# Snow Painting

**MATERIALS NEEDED:**
Dark-colored construction paper
Crayons
Hot water
Epsom salts
Bowls
Paintbrushes
Measuring cups and spoons

**MIXTURE (PER CHILD):**
¼ cup hot water
4 tablespoons Epsom salts

Stir hot water and Epsom salts together in a bowl until salts are dissolved.

**PROCEDURE:**
- Give each child a sheet of paper.
- Allow the children to draw freely with crayons on the paper.
- When drawings are complete, have the children paint the paper with the salt mixture.
- Let the drawings dry to see the snowy effect.

# Crayon Stained Glass

**MATERIALS NEEDED:**
Waxed paper
Crayons
Cheese grater, pencil sharpener, or butter knife (for adult use only)
Scissors
Electric iron (for adult use only)
String, ribbon, or yarn
Hole punch

**PROCEDURE:**
- Guide the children in cutting two squares of waxed paper.
- Create crayon shavings using a cheese grater, pencil sharpener, or butter knife. Only an adult should complete this step.
- Have the children sprinkle crayon shavings onto one square of their waxed paper.
- Place the second sheet of waxed paper on top of the piece containing the crayon shavings.
- Use the iron to fuse the sheets of waxed paper together, creating the stained glass look. Only an adult should use the iron.
- Once the waxed paper is fused together, use the hole punch and string to create a hanger for the stained glass.
- Display the final projects in a window.

# Sandpaper Crayon Art

**MATERIALS NEEDED:**
Sandpaper (medium grade)
Crayons
Electric iron (for adult use only)

**PROCEDURE:**
- Give each child a piece of sandpaper.
- Have the children use crayons to create a drawing on the sandpaper.
- Use an iron to heat the top of the sandpaper drawing, and watch the crayons melt into the sand. Only an adult should complete this step.

# Crayon Resist Drawings

**MATERIALS NEEDED:**
White paper
Crayons
Black shoe polish
Black liquid tempera paint
Sponges
Paintbrushes
Toothpicks

**PROCEDURE:**
- Give each child a piece of paper.
- Have the children use the crayons to cover the entire paper with a variety of colors.
- Next, the children should use sponges to completely cover their paper with a layer of black shoe polish.
- The children should then use paintbrushes to apply a layer of black liquid tempera paint.
- Have the children use toothpicks to scratch designs or drawings into the black layers. As they scratch, the color of the crayons will shine through.

# Crayon Glue Rubbing

**MATERIALS NEEDED:**
White paper
Peeled crayons (Thicker crayons are best.)
White school glue

**PROCEDURE:**
- Give each child a sheet of white paper.
- Have the children use the white school glue to create a design or drawing on their paper.
- Once the glue is dry, place the glue drawing under a second sheet of white paper.
- Next, have the children rub the top sheet of paper with the side of a crayon.
- The glue design or drawing will show through on the paper as a print.

# PART 3

# Collage and Sculpture

# Collage

**MATERIALS NEEDED:**
Matte board, canvas, wood, or paper plate
White school glue
Bowls
Glue brushes
Collage materials*

**PROCEDURE:**
- Each child should have a matte board, canvas, or other collage base and a glue bowl and brush.
- Place a variety of collage materials on the table. Do not give the children the materials to glue, but rather let them make their own choices about which materials to use.
- Have the children brush white school glue onto their base and stick on collage materials freely. Materials may be glued on top of one another for an overlapping effect.

* Examples of collage materials: fabric, shapes, cotton balls, jewelry, large buttons, corks, bottle caps, spools, cylinders, shells, rocks, seeds, and pinecones.

# Create Your Own Poster

**MATERIALS NEEDED:**
Poster board or cardboard
Magazines
White school glue
Bowls
Glue brushes
Scissors

**PROCEDURE:**
- Let the children look through magazines and tear or cut up pictures. This works well when children are given a specific topic—for example, animals.
- Once the children have several pictures of their topic, they can use the white school glue and brushes to attach the pictures to their boards.
- Eventually, the images will overlap and children will have an interesting poster.

# Fabric Mobiles

**MATERIALS NEEDED:**
Fabric swatches
Clear plastic lids
White school glue
Bowls
Glue brushes
Hole punch
Yarn

**PROCEDURE:**
- Have plenty of fabric swatches available. Allow each child to choose several.
- Give each child a clear plastic lid.
- Have the children use a glue brush to cover their lid with white school glue.
- Allow the children to place fabric swatches on the glue.
- Punch a hole in the fabric-covered lids, and assist the children in attaching a length of yarn for hanging.

# Nature Collage

**MATERIALS NEEDED:**
Small pieces of wood, about 5 inches square (A roof shingle cut into 2 or 3 pieces works well.)
Pinecones and acorns
White school glue
Squeeze bottles or bowls and glue brushes
Staghorn lichen (optional)

**PROCEDURE:**
- Allow each child to select a piece of wood.
- Have the children squeeze or brush glue generously over the wood.
- Allow the children to select pinecones or acorns and arrange them on the wood until the area is fully covered.

Optional: Use staghorn lichen to fill empty areas. For a sheen, paint entire collage with watered-down glue.

# String and Glue Art

**MATERIALS NEEDED:**
Dark-colored paper or matte board
String and yarn (various thicknesses)
White school glue thinned with water
Bowls

**PROCEDURE:**
- Have small bowls of watered-down glue on hand for each child at the table.
- Cut string or yarn into pieces.
- Give each child a piece of paper or matte board.
- Have the children dip yarn or string pieces into glue. Have them pull the pieces between their fingers to get rid of excess glue.
- Children should arrange the dipped yarn or string into a design on their paper or matte board.

# String and Paint

**MATERIALS NEEDED:**
White paper or matte board
Liquid tempera paint
String and yarn (various thicknesses)
Bowls

**PROCEDURE:**
- Have small bowls of liquid tempera paint in a variety of colors available at each table.
- Cut string or yarn into pieces.
- Give each child a piece of white paper or white matte board.
- Have the children dip yarn or string pieces into liquid tempera paint. Have them pull the pieces between their fingers to get rid of excess paint.
- Children should arrange the dipped yarn or string into a design on their paper or matte board.

# Foam Sculptures

**MATERIALS NEEDED:**
Toothpicks
Foam core cut into small pieces or foam cubes

**PROCEDURE:**
- Have children create sculptures by putting toothpicks into foam pieces, creating a design similar to a Tinkertoy.
- The toothpicks will hold the foam pieces in place so the sculpture is mobile, and the children can take their creations home.

# Wire Sculpture

**MATERIALS NEEDED:**
Empty half-pint milk cartons (one per child)
Plaster of paris
Water
Coated electrical wire cut into various lengths
Watercolor paints
Paintbrushes
Bowl
Mixing spoon
Measuring cup

> **MIXTURE:**
> 2 cups plaster of paris
> 1 cup water

Mix together. Makes enough for six milk cartons.

**PROCEDURE:**
- Pour mixed plaster of paris into the milk cartons. Give each child a carton.
- As the plaster begins to set, have the children place the ends of the wires into the plaster in any arrangement.
- Let the plaster set, and then have the children remove the milk cartons by tearing them away from the plaster.
- After the milk cartons are removed, the children may then move the wires into any shape or sculpture.
- Once the sculptures are complete, the plaster bases may be painted.

# Free-Form Mobile

**MATERIALS NEEDED:**

White tissue paper, 10 x 12 inches
Yarn, cut in 36-inch lengths
Watercolors
White school glue
Liquid starch
Small bowl
Paintbrushes
Scissors
Black thread and needle (for adult use only)

**PROCEDURE:**

**Day 1**

- Mix together 2 parts white school glue and 1 part liquid starch in a small bowl.
- Give each child two sheets of white tissue paper and one length of yarn.
- Have the children tie the two ends of yarn together, forming a circle.
- Let the children dip their yarn into the glue/starch mixture. Have them run their fingers down the yarn to squeeze out excess liquid.

- Have the children place their yarn on one sheet of the tissue paper, making the shape they want.
- Place the second sheet of tissue paper on top of the yarn figure, and have the children gently press down where yarn touches the tissue.
- Set aside to dry.

**Day 2**

- Have the children cut the tissue paper around the outside of the yarn shape.
- Allow the children to use paintbrushes to paint the tissue paper with watercolor. Using too much water may cause the tissue paper to dissolve.

- Once the tissue paper dries, poke a needle and thread through the tissue (to be done only by an adult).
- Tie the thread to hang the artwork.

# Plastic Sculpture

**MATERIALS NEEDED:**
Matte board, cardboard, or other sturdy material
Liquid tempera paint
Plaster of paris
Water
Styrofoam pieces, sawdust, or shredded paper
Containers for plaster (large and small)
Bowls
Paintbrushes
Spoons
Bucket

**PROCEDURE:**

- Mix only enough plaster of paris for two or three children to use at one time.
- Mix approximately 1 cup dry plaster to ½ cup water per child in one large container. (Don't overmix, as plaster will set up quickly.)
- Add Styrofoam pieces, shredded paper, sawdust, or anything that will add bulk to the plaster.
- Give each child a matte board or other base and an equal portion of the plaster mixture in an individual container.
- Let the children scoop plaster onto their base as they wish.
- Once the children are finished, have them wash their hands in the bucket of water. Wash all utensils and containers in the bucket also and not in the sink. The plaster mixture can clog the sink drain.
- Let sculptures dry.
- Once the sculptures are dry, allow the children to paint them with liquid tempera paint.

# Sand Drawing

**MATERIALS NEEDED:**
Matte board, cardboard, or paper plate
Powdered tempera paint
Sand
White school glue in squeeze bottles
Bowls
Spoons

**PROCEDURE:**

- Mix 1 teaspoon powdered tempera with $\frac{2}{3}$ cup sand. Make this mixture in separate bowls with three or four different colors.
- Give each child a piece of cardboard, matte board, or a paper plate.
- Have the children squeeze glue onto the board to draw a design.
- Allow them to sprinkle colored sand onto the glue, then shake off excess sand.

# Shape Collage

**MATERIALS NEEDED:**
Matte board, cardboard, or other sturdy material in various shapes
Paper, fabric, plastic, or Styrofoam cut into smaller shapes
White school glue
Bowls
Glue brushes

**PROCEDURE:**

- Allow the children to choose which shape board they prefer to work with.
- Have the children brush the glue onto various smaller shapes and then attach them to the board.
- Do not interfere with children's choice of shapes and materials.

# Pretzel Art

**MATERIALS NEEDED:**
Pretzel dough ingredients (See mixture below.)
Store-bought pretzels of various shapes and sizes
Bowls
Mixing spoons
Measuring cups and spoons

**MIXTURE:**
1 package yeast
1 tablespoon sugar
1½ cups warm water
1 teaspoon salt
4–5 cups whole wheat flour
4 cups grated sharp cheddar cheese

Dissolve yeast and sugar in warm water. Combine salt, 4 cups flour, and cheese. Stir in yeast mixture. Knead 5 to 10 minutes, adding flour a little at a time until dough is no longer sticky but smooth.

**PROCEDURE:**
- Give each child a ball of pretzel dough.
- Have bowls of store-bought pretzels of various shapes and sizes available on the table.
- Have the children create sculptures using dough to connect pretzels.
- Once the sculptures are finished, bake at 475° for 10 minutes, and eat when cooled.

# Paper Strip Sculpture

## MATERIALS NEEDED:

Matte board, cardboard, or other sturdy material
Strips of white paper cut to various lengths
Liquid watercolors
Water
Liquid starch (optional)
White school glue
Bowls
Glue brushes

## PROCEDURE:

- Add drops of liquid watercolors to bowls of water. Use a small amount of water and a lot of liquid watercolors.
- Let the children dye strips of paper with liquid watercolors by stirring the paper strips around in colored water until the color dyes the paper.
- Hang strips on a drying rack and let the strips dry completely.
- Have the children glue colored paper strips to their boards. The strips can be built up, piled, and connected.
- Let dry.

Optional: If you want the paper to be a little stiff, put some liquid starch into the colored water.

# Smelly Collage

## MATERIALS NEEDED:

Matte board, cardboard, or other sturdy material
Perfume, spices, potpourri, toothpaste, soap, and other items that have a scent
Facial tissues
White school glue

## PROCEDURE:

- Lay out scented materials on the table.
- Give each child a matte board or other base.
- Have the children glue the scented materials onto their base.
- Facial tissues can be used for the liquid items, such as perfume, and then glued down.
- Let collage dry, and smell.

# Sandwich Collage

**MATERIALS NEEDED:**
Newspaper or cardboard
Construction paper
Colored cellophane
Ferns (dried and flattened)
Tissue paper
Wrapping paper
Photograph mounting paper
Waxed paper
Electric iron (for adult use only)

**PROCEDURE:**

- Cut the cellophane and photo mounting paper to fit the size of the construction paper. Cut waxed paper slightly larger than the construction paper.
- Have children rip the tissue paper and wrapping paper into small pieces.
- Place a piece of cardboard or newspaper on a hard surface.
- Place a piece of construction paper on top of the cardboard or newspaper.
- Finally, place a sheet of colored cellophane onto the construction paper.
- Let the children lay out the dried ferns and, if they like, some tissue or wrapping paper (face down).
- Guide them to place a piece of photograph mounting paper over the cellophane and dried-fern design.
- Cover each design with a piece of waxed paper.
- Run an iron set on low heat—no steam—over the waxed paper. Press down and heat as long as it takes to adhere the mounting paper, about 30 seconds to a minute. An adult should complete this step.
- Let cool, and remove the construction paper.
- Turn the artwork over and trim excess waxed paper.

# Egg Carton Sculpture

**MATERIALS NEEDED:**
Matte board, cardboard, or other sturdy material
Egg cartons cut into individual cups
White school glue
Liquid tempera paint
Paintbrushes

**PROCEDURE:**
- Give each child a piece of matte board, cardboard, or other base material
- Allow the children to glue egg carton cups freely onto their base.
- Once glue is dry, have them use tempera paint to add color to their sculptures.

# Fruit Seed Collage

**MATERIALS NEEDED:**
Matte board, cardboard, paper plates, or other sturdy material
All types of fruit seeds (melons, pumpkins, apples, oranges, papaya, peaches, or plums)
White school glue
Bowls
Glue brushes

**PROCEDURE:**
- Give each child a piece of matte board, cardboard, or other base material.
- Allow the children to glue the various fruit seeds freely onto their base.

Note: This activity is great for language development. Discuss the various kinds of fruits from which the seeds come. Real fruit or pictures of fruit would enhance this experience for young children.

# Ice Sculpture

**MATERIALS NEEDED:**
Water table or deep basin
30–50 pounds of ice cubes
Liquid watercolors
Rock salt
Water
Bowls
Eyedroppers

**PROCEDURE:**
- Dump ice cubes into the water table or basin.
- Pour some rock salt over the ice.
- Add drops of liquid watercolors to bowls filled with water, and place the bowls and eyedroppers around the table.
- Allow the children to drip the colored water onto the ice to create beautiful ice designs. Encourage the children to blend colors and watch new colors emerge.

# Tissue Collage

**MATERIALS NEEDED:**
Matte board, cardboard, or other sturdy material
Tissue paper scraps
White school glue thinned with water
Markers (Thick, black water-based markers are best.)
Bowls
Paintbrushes

**PROCEDURE:**
- Give each child a matte board or other base material.
- Let the children apply the glue to the base using their fingers or paintbrushes.
- Have them arrange the tissue paper scraps in any design desired. It is fine if they overlap pieces.
- Allow the glue to dry for a few minutes.
- Once the glue is dry, let the children draw on the tissue paper with markers.
- Let dry, and cover the drawings with a thin layer of watered-down glue to set it.

· · · · · · · · · · · · · · · · · · · · · · · · · · · · · · · · · · · · · · · · · · · · · · · · · · · ·

# Sea Life Collage

**MATERIALS NEEDED:**

Blue base material (to symbolize the ocean): matte board, paper, or plastic plates
Beach items: seaweed, feathers, shells, sand, driftwood, starfish, sand dollars, corks
White school glue
Bowls
Glue brushes

**PROCEDURE:**

- Give each child a blue base material.
- Allow the children to select their own beach items for their collage.
- Have them use glue brushes and glue to attach their items to the base.

· · · · · · · · · · · · · · · · · · · · · · · · · · · · · · · · · · · · · · · · · · · · · · · · · · · ·

# Colored Styrofoam and Toothpick Sculpture

**MATERIALS NEEDED:**

Styrofoam, broken into small bits
Liquid tempera paint
Colored toothpicks
White school glue
Bowls
Spoons
Newspaper

**PROCEDURE:**

- Place Styrofoam pieces into several bowls and add liquid tempera paint.
- Let the children use spoons to stir the Styrofoam around until the foam is colored.
- Place the colored Styrofoam on newspaper and allow it to dry.
- When Styrofoam is dry, have the children dip the ends of the toothpicks into glue and then into the Styrofoam.
- This will create a Tinkertoy kind of sculpture.

Note: When the glue dries, sculptures will not fall apart and can be picked up and taken home.

# Free-Form Plastic Bag Sculpture

**MATERIALS NEEDED:**
Thick, sturdy plastic sandwich bags
Plaster of paris
Water
Bowls
Spoons
Measuring cups
Twist ties

**PROCEDURE:**

- Give each child a plastic bag, a bowl of dry plaster of paris, and a bowl of water.
- Have each child use spoons to measure 1 cup of plaster of paris and ½ cup of water. Have the children pour the plaster and water into their bags.
- Put twist ties onto the bags to seal them shut.
- Let the children knead, roll, or punch the bags of plaster.
- As they work with it, the plaster will start to set.
- Once the plaster of paris is hard, remove the bags to reveal unique free-form sculptures.

# Paper Tube Sculpture

**MATERIALS NEEDED:**
Paper tubes from paper towels, toilet paper, or wrapping paper
White school glue
Scissors
Hole punch
Straws (optional)

**PROCEDURE:**

- Cut the paper tubes into various lengths, and use a hole punch to cut designs into them. Cut spirals, negative space, and other shapes into the tubes.
- Let the children arrange and connect the paper tubes as desired using glue.
- The tubes can be stacked, fitted inside of each other, used as bridges, and arranged in other combinations.

Optional: Straws can be added to create a different look.

# Mud Brick Sculpture

**MATERIALS NEEDED FOR BRICKS:**
Dirt
Water
Mixing bowl
Ice cube trays or muffin tins

**PROCEDURE FOR MAKING BRICKS:**
- Put dirt into the bowl.
- Add some water.
- Mix the mud to a consistency where you can form it into a ball.
- Press the mud into an ice cube tray or muffin tin.
- Put the trays in a warm place.
- Let the bricks dry for about 10 days, or bake them in a 250°oven for 15 minutes.
- Do the drop test: Slip a brick out of the tray and drop it onto the floor. If it doesn't break, the bricks are dry enough.

**MATERIALS NEEDED FOR SCULPTURE:**
Matte board or other sturdy material
Mud bricks
Rocks or pebbles, wood, sticks, leaves, or other nature treasures
Mud or plaster of paris mixed to a runny consistency

**PROCEDURE FOR SCULPTURE:**
- Give each child a matte board or other base material.
- Allow the children to freely explore and build using the various materials.
- The mud or plaster of paris can be used to stick the materials together.
- Let dry.

# Confetti Collage

**MATERIALS NEEDED:**

White paper

Construction paper in a variety of colors

Bowls

Glitter

White school glue

Cotton swabs

Toothpicks

Scissors

Hole punch

Guide the children to help make confetti. There are two ways to do this:

1. Let them use a hole punch to punch holes into various colors of construction paper. The holes become confetti.

2. Cut construction paper into thin strips, and then let the children cut or tear the strips to make confetti.

**PROCEDURE:**

- Once the confetti has been created, let the children choose two colors of confetti. Have them put their confetti into a bowl and mix it with a toothpick.
- Give each child a sheet of white paper.

- Have the children use a cotton swab dipped in glue to make a design on the paper.
- Next, have children sprinkle their drawings with confetti and glitter.
- Finally, shake off the excess glitter and confetti, and let the drawings dry.

# Sawdust Sculptures

**MATERIALS NEEDED:**
Liquid tempera paint
Sawdust
Wheat paste
Water
Container for sawdust mixture
Paintbrushes
Mixing spoons
Measuring cups

**MIXTURE (PER CHILD):**
4 cups sawdust
1 cup wheat paste
2 cups water
Mix sawdust, wheat paste, and water together in large container.

**PROCEDURE:**
- Give each child a lump of the sawdust mixture to mold into a free-form sculpture.
- Allow the sculptures to dry at least 24 hours.
- Once the sculptures are dry, have the children paint their sculptures with liquid tempera paint.

# PART 4

# Modeling Materials

# Clay Play

**MATERIALS NEEDED:**
Clay
Tools to use for shaping and molding clay

**PROCEDURE:**
- Put a pile of clay on the table for each child.
- Try to vary the availability of tools—some days allow hands only, other days put out clay molding tools.
- Encourage the children's pounding, rolling, poking, and smashing of the clay.
- Be sure to put clay back into plastic bags or containers each day for storage.

# Baker's Dough

**MATERIALS NEEDED:**
Flour
Water
Liquid watercolors or liquid tempera paint
Bowls
Mixing spoons
Measuring spoons and cups

**MIXTURE (PER CHILD):**
1 cup flour
½ cup water
2 squirts of liquid watercolors or 1 teaspoon liquid tempera paint
Stir all ingredients together. Mixture should be consistency of playdough.

**PROCEDURE:**
- Allow the children to play and create with, mold, pound, and stir the dough.
- If dough is sticking to hands, have a small bowl of flour available. Children should pat their hands with flour.

Note: To save the sculptures, let dough air-dry for 24 hours.

# Cooked Clay

**MATERIALS NEEDED:**
Salt
Water
Liquid watercolors or liquid tempera paint
Cornstarch
Bowls
Mixing spoons
Measuring cups and spoons
Saucepan
Hot plate or stove (adult use only)

### MIXTURE:
2/3 cup water
1 teaspoon liquid tempera paint or 2 squirts of liquid watercolors
2 cups salt
1 cup cornstarch
1/2 cup cold water

An adult should complete these steps. Add 1 teaspoon liquid tempera paint or 2 squirts of liquid watercolors to 2/3 cup water. Mix salt and colored water together in saucepan and stir over medium heat for 3 to 4 minutes. Remove mixture from heat and add cornstarch and 1/2 cup cold water. Stir until smooth.

**PROCEDURE:**
- When the mixture has cooled, give the children a lump of clay, and let them play freely.
- Encourage the children's pounding, rolling, poking, and smashing of the clay.
- Be sure to put clay back into plastic bags or containers each day for storage.

Note: Clay will not keep for more than a few days.

# Moon Craters

**MATERIALS NEEDED:**
Matte board, cardboard, or other sturdy material
Liquid starch
Rock salt
White school glue
Liquid watercolors or liquid tempera paint
Bowls
Mixing spoons
Measuring cups and spoons

**MIXTURE (PER CHILD):**
½ cup liquid starch
2 cups rock salt
½ cup glue
2 squirts of liquid watercolors or 1 teaspoon liquid tempera paint

Combine all ingredients. Once mixed, this makes a gooey, rocky mixture.

**PROCEDURE:**
- Give each child a matte board or cardboard to use as a base.
- Let the children freely pile clay onto the boards to create 3-D structures.
- Once the sculptures are complete, allow them to dry. The mixture will crystallize and dry hard.

# Detergent Painting

**MATERIALS NEEDED:**
Matte board, cardboard, or other sturdy material
Liquid detergent
Water
Liquid watercolors or liquid tempera paint
Bowls
Spoons
Measuring cups
Eggbeater

**MIXTURE (PER CHILD):**
1 cup liquid detergent
⅛ cup water
1 teaspoon liquid tempera paint or 2 squirts of liquid watercolors

Beat mixture with eggbeater until smooth, shiny, and stiff.

**PROCEDURE:**
- Give each child a matte board or cardboard to use as a base.
- Let the children pile the mixture onto the base material. It will stick and pile up.

# Goop

**MATERIALS NEEDED:**
Cornstarch
Water
Liquid watercolors or liquid tempera paint
Trays
Bowls
Spoons
Measuring cups

**MIXTURE (PER CHILD):**
1/2 cup cornstarch
1/4 cup water
2 squirts of liquid watercolors or 1 teaspoon liquid tempera paint

Stir all ingredients together.

**PROCEDURE:**
- Pour this mixture onto a tray for each child.
- Allow the children to experiment with the goop.
- Add more cornstarch. What happens? More water. What happens?
- This is a tactile experience and not to be taken home.

Note: Mixture can be saved for future use.

# Oily Dough

**MATERIALS NEEDED:**
Flour
Vegetable oil
Water
Liquid watercolors or liquid tempera paint
Bowls
Spoons
Measuring cups
Aprons or smocks

**MIXTURE:**
4 cups flour
1 cup vegetable oil
1 cup water
2 squirts of liquid watercolors or 1 teaspoon liquid tempera paint

Knead mixture together.

**PROCEDURE:**
- Allow children to play freely with the mixture.

Note: This dough is oily. Therefore, wearing aprons is advised, and children should wash their hands afterward.

# Cornstarch Modeling Mixture

**MATERIALS NEEDED:**
Salt
Cornstarch
Water
Liquid watercolors or liquid tempera paint
Saucepan
Mixing spoons
Measuring cups
Hot plate or stove (for adult use only)

**MIXTURE (PER CHILD):**
½ cup water
1 cup salt
½ cup cornstarch
Liquid watercolors or liquid tempera paint

An adult should complete these steps. Bring water to a boil in medium saucepan. Mix in salt, cornstarch, and liquid watercolors or liquid tempera paint. Heat mixture over low heat, stirring continuously until mixture is too stiff to stir. Remove from heat and cool. Knead mixture until smooth.

**PROCEDURE:**
• Give each child a lump of modeling clay to play with freely.

Note: This modeling mixture will not dry well.

# Sawdust Mixture:

**MATERIALS NEEDED:**
Sawdust
Wheat paste
Water
Liquid watercolors or liquid tempera paint (optional)
Bowls
Mixing spoons
Measuring cups
Liquid tempera paint (alternate)
Paintbrushes (alternate)

**MIXTURE (PER CHILD):**
4 cups sawdust
1 cup wheat paste
2½ cups water
1 teaspoon liquid tempera paint or 2 squirts of liquid watercolors (optional)

Stir together sawdust, wheat paste, and water. Add liquid tempera paint or liquid watercolors, if desired.

**PROCEDURE:**
- Give each child some sawdust mixture to play with freely.
- Allow the mixture to harden and dry to create sculptures.

Variation: If you do not add color when creating the mixture, the dough can be painted when dry.

# Soap Dough

**MATERIALS NEEDED:**
Salt
Liquid starch
Liquid soap
Water
White school glue
Cornmeal
Bowls
Mixing spoons
Measuring cups
Measuring spoons

**MIXTURE:**
4 tablespoons salt
½ cup liquid starch
1 cup liquid soap
⅛ cup water
1 tablespoon glue
2 cups cornmeal

Stir ingredients together in large bowl. To this mixture add:
½ cup glue
1½ cups cornmeal

Mix all ingredients.

**PROCEDURE:**
• Give each child a lump of soap dough to
  play with freely.

# Toothpaste Putty

**MATERIALS NEEDED:**
Toothpaste (cream, not gel)
White school glue
Cornstarch
Water
Small bowl
Mixing spoons
Measuring spoons

**MIXTURE (PER CHILD):**
½ teaspoon toothpaste
1 tablespoon white school glue
2 tablespoons cornstarch
½ teaspoon water

Mix toothpaste, glue, and cornstarch in small bowl. Add water. Mix dough until it's like putty.

**PROCEDURE:**
- Let children push, pull, roll, and play freely with the putty.

Note: Putty begins to dry in 20 minutes, so to soften it, use a drop of water. Putty will dry hard in 24 hours.

# Fun Dough

**MATERIALS NEEDED:**
Flour
Salt
Water
Liquid watercolors or liquid tempera paint
Vegetable oil
Vinegar
Bowls
Mixing spoons
Measuring cups and spoons

## MIXTURE:
1 cup water
Liquid watercolors or liquid tempera paint
3 cups flour
1 cup salt
¼ cup vegetable oil
2 tablespoons vinegar

Add liquid watercolors or liquid tempera paint to 1 cup water. Add flour, salt, vegetable oil, and vinegar to colored water. Mix all ingredients well. Add more water if too dry. Knead mixture to dough-like consistency.

## PROCEDURE:
• Let the children play freely with the dough.

Note: This dough keeps indefinitely in a plastic bag. Dampen occasionally by working water into the dough as it dries out.

# Kool-Aid Playdough

**MATERIALS NEEDED:**
Water
Flour
Salt
Vegetable oil
Unsweetened Kool-Aid drink mix
Bowl
Measuring cups and spoons
Mixing spoons
Hot plate or stove (for adult use only)

**MIXTURE:**
2 cups water
2½ cups flour
1 cup salt
2 packages Kool-Aid drink mix
3 teaspoons vegetable oil

These steps should be done only by an adult. Bring 2 cups water to a boil. Mix dry ingredients in bowl. Add boiling water and oil to dry mixture. Knead mixture to dough-like consistency.

**PROCEDURE:**
- Give each child a lump of dough to play with freely.

# Salt and Starch Modeling Mixture

**MATERIALS NEEDED:**
Salt
Cornstarch
Water
Liquid tempera paint
Paintbrushes
Double boiler (for adult use only)
Hot plate or stove
Waxed paper or cookie sheet
Measuring cups
Mixing spoons

**MIXTURE (PER CHILD):**
1 cup salt
½ cup cornstarch
¾ cup cold water

These steps should be done only by an adult. Fill bottom of double boiler with water and bring to a boil. Mix salt and cornstarch in top of double boiler. Add cold water slowly while stirring continuously. Stir mixture until well combined. Place pan over boiling water and stir mixture constantly until it has thickened and is difficult to stir. Spoon dough onto waxed paper or cookie sheet to cool. Knead dough a bit to take out air bubbles and lumps.

**PROCEDURE:**
- Give each child a lump of modeling clay to play with freely.
- This dough will dry, and the children can paint their dough creations once they are dry.

Note: When not using modeling material, roll it into a ball and wrap well in waxed paper. It will remain soft for several days.

# Modeling Dough

**MATERIALS NEEDED:**

Flour

Salt

Powdered alum or oil of cloves (both items available at a pharmacy)

Vegetable oil

Water

Liquid watercolors or liquid tempera paint

Paintbrushes

Bowls

Saucepan

Hot plate or stove (adult use only)

Measuring cups and spoons

Mixing spoons

**MIXTURE (PER CHILD):**

$\frac{1}{2}$ cup water

$\frac{3}{4}$ cup flour

$\frac{1}{2}$ cup salt

$1\frac{1}{2}$ teaspoons powdered alum or oil of cloves

$1\frac{1}{2}$ teaspoons vegetable oil

Liquid watercolors or liquid tempera paint

Only an adult should complete these steps. Heat $\frac{1}{2}$ cup water in saucepan until boiling. Mix flour, salt, and alum or oil of cloves in mixing bowl. Add vegetable oil and boiling water to flour mixture. Stir vigorously with spoon until well blended. Dough should not stick to sides of bowl (add more flour if necessary) and should be cool enough to handle. Add liquid watercolors or liquid tempera paint and knead coloring into dough.

**PROCEDURE:**

- Give each child a lump of modeling dough to play with freely.
- Let the children's creations dry overnight.
- Have the children paint their work once it has dried.

# Craft Clay

**MATERIALS NEEDED:**
Cornstarch
Baking soda
Water
Liquid watercolors
Measuring cups
Mixing spoons
Hot plate or stove (adult use only)
Saucepan
Cookie sheet
Liquid tempera paint (optional)
Paintbrushes (optional)
White school glue thinned with water (optional)

**MIXTURE (PER CHILD):**
1 cup cornstarch
2 cups baking soda
1¼ cup water
Liquid watercolors

These steps should be completed only by an adult. Combine all ingredients in saucepan. Cook over medium heat, stirring continuously. Dump mixture onto cookie sheet to cool. Knead mixture while it is cooling.

**PROCEDURE:**
• When the clay is cool, give each child a lump of clay to play with freely.

Note: Store clay in foil or in an airtight container.

Optional: This mixture will harden and can then be painted. After it has been painted, a final coat of watered-down glue will give it a shine.

# Cloud Dough

**MATERIALS NEEDED:**
Flour
Powdered tempera paint
Vegetable oil
Bowl
Water
Mixing spoons
Measuring cups and spoons

**MIXTURE:**
3 cups flour
2 tablespoons powdered tempera paint
½ cup vegetable oil
Water

Mix together flour, powdered tempera paint, and oil. Add enough water to make soft, pliable, elastic-like dough.

**PROCEDURE:**
- Give each child a lump of dough to play with freely.

# Sand Sculptures

**MATERIALS NEEDED:**
Waxed paper
Plaster of paris
Sand
Liquid tempera paint
Water
Paintbrushes
Mixing bowl
Mixing spoons

**PROCEDURE:**

- Give each child a sheet of waxed paper.
- Allow the children to mix water and plaster of paris together in a mixing bowl until it looks like cream.
- Next, have them quickly stir in the sand until the mixture looks like thick whipped cream.
- Have the children pour some of the mixture onto their waxed paper, creating gullies, valleys, and hills. Allow them to squeeze and push the mixture to make designs.
- This mixture dries very quickly (about 5 minutes).
- Have the children paint their sand sculptures once they are dry.

# PART 5

# Chalk

# Chalk and Wet Paper

**MATERIALS NEEDED:**
White paper
Wet sponge
Chalk

**PROCEDURE:**
- Give each child a sheet of paper.
- Children should wet their paper slightly with a wrung-out sponge.
- Have the children draw freely on their wet paper with colored chalk. Show them how to use the sides and ends of the chalk to create different designs.
- Allow the paper to dry.

# Chalk Screening

**MATERIALS NEEDED:**
Large, colored construction paper
Cornstarch
Water
Chalk
Paintbrushes
Small wire mesh screening
Small bowls
Mixing spoons
Stencils (optional)

**PROCEDURE:**
- Give each child a sheet of construction paper.
- Fill bowls one-third full with cornstarch and mix in water. This should be a thin liquid.
- Have the children paint with the cornstarch mixture on their construction paper.
- Place wire screening on top of the construction paper.
- Allow the children to draw with chalk on top of the wire mesh.
- Cornstarch mixture will allow the chalk to adhere to the paper.

Optional: Stencils or patterns can be placed between the cornstarch mixture and mesh to create a negative print.

# Grated Chalk and Water

**MATERIALS NEEDED:**
White paper
Colored chalk
Dishpan
Water
Grater (for adult use only)

**PROCEDURE:**

- Adult should grate various colors of chalk ahead of time to create chalk shavings.
- Fill the dishpan with just enough water to cover bottom.
- Let the children place grated chalk on top of the water. Do not stir.
- Give each child a sheet of paper.
- Have the children lay their paper on top of the chalk and water.
- Pull the paper off and allow to dry.

# Cotton Swab Chalk Design

**MATERIALS NEEDED:**
White paper
Colored chalk
Water
Cups, muffin tins, egg cartons, or any container to separate colors
Cotton swabs
Small bowls
Potato peeler, cheese grater, or pencil sharpener (for adult use only)

**PROCEDURE:**

- Adult should grate colored chalk into cups, muffin tins, egg cartons, or any container to separate the colors.
- Place small bowls of water and cotton swabs on the table.
- Give each child a sheet of paper.
- Have the children dip a cotton swab into the water, and then into the chalk and draw freely using the swab as a paintbrush.

# Chalk and Finger Painting

**MATERIALS NEEDED:**
Light-colored construction paper
Trays
Chalk
Fingerpaint

**PROCEDURE:**
- Give each child a sheet of light-colored construction paper.
- Allow the children to freely draw with colored chalk on the paper.
- Set the chalk drawings aside.
- Have the children spread fingerpaint on trays.
- Children should then wash and dry their hands.
- Finally, have the children press their chalk drawings onto their fingerpainted trays to allow the transfer of paint onto their drawings.

# Chalk Painting

**MATERIALS NEEDED:**
White paper
Colored chalk
Water
Small sponges or paintbrushes
Potato peeler, cheese grater, or pencil sharpener (for adult use only)
Small bowls

**PROCEDURE:**
- Finely grate colored chalk into separate bowls. (This step should be completed by an adult.) Each bowl should hold one color.
- Supply each child with a piece of paper, a bowl of water, and a variety of small sponges or paintbrushes.
- Let the children dip their sponges into the water and then into the desired color of grated chalk.
- Have them use their dipped sponges to paint freely on their paper.
- The colors will mix and change as children continue to paint.

# Chalk and Tempera

**MATERIALS NEEDED:**
White paper
Colored chalk
White liquid tempera paint
Paintbrushes

**PROCEDURE:**
- Give each child a sheet of paper.
- Have the children make a colored chalk drawing on their piece of paper. Be sure they press down hard with the chalk.
- Next, have each child take another piece of paper of the same size and brush white liquid tempera paint over the entire surface.
- While the paint is still wet, have the children place the chalk drawing face down on top of the painted paper and press.
- Lift off the top piece and see the results.

# Chalk Presentation

**MATERIALS NEEDED:**
Sandpaper—medium to fine grade
Colored chalk
Small bowls
White school glue thinned with water
Construction paper (alternate)

**PROCEDURE:**
- Give each child a sheet of sandpaper, colored chalk, and a bowl of thinned white school glue.
- Have the children dip the chalk into the glue and draw freely on their sandpaper.

Variation: Construction paper can be used instead of sandpaper.

# Grated Chalk and Stencils

**MATERIALS NEEDED:**
White paper
Colored chalk
Wet sponge
Saltshakers with large holes
Potato peeler, cheese grater, or pencil sharpener (for adult use only)
Hairspray (optional) (for adult use only)
Watercolor paint (alternate)
Paintbrushes (alternate)

**PROCEDURE:**

- An adult should grate various colors of chalk ahead of time to create chalk shavings.
- Transfer grated chalk into saltshakers.
- Give each child a sheet of paper.
- Have the children use a wrung-out wet sponge to wet their paper completely.
- Then have children *shake, shake, shake* the chalk onto the wet paper.

Optional: Let the creations dry, and when the children have left the room, use hairspray to set the chalk.

Variation: On heavier paper, the children can paint a thin layer of watercolor paint on the paper and then shake on the chalk.

# Sponge and Chalk Prints

**MATERIALS NEEDED:**
White paper
Wet sponges
Chalk

**PROCEDURE:**

- Give each child a sheet of paper and a wet sponge.
- Allow the children to draw freely on the wet sponges with a piece of chalk.
- Once the sponges are covered in chalk, have the children dab them on their paper and see the chalk print.

# Paper Towel and Chalk

**MATERIALS NEEDED:**
Large, shallow pan
Water
Heavy-duty paper towels
Chalk in various colors

**PROCEDURE:**
- Give each child a sheet of paper towel.
- Have the children dip the towels into a pan of water and wring them out.
- Place the wet paper towels on a table and smooth out the wrinkles.
- Let the children draw on their damp paper towels with chalk.

# Liquid Starch and Chalk

**MATERIALS NEEDED:**
White paper
Liquid starch
Paintbrushes
Water
Bowl
Chalk
Smocks or aprons

**PROCEDURE:**
- Give each child a piece of paper.

There are two ways to have the children create designs:

- Have the children use paintbrushes to paint the entire paper with liquid starch, and then draw on the paper with chalk.
- Have the children dip chalk into a bowl of liquid starch and use the chalk to draw on the paper.

Let children freely experiment with either method. If too much starch is used, you may need to wipe some off or the project can get too messy and can frustrate the children. Show the children how to use the ends and sides of the chalk to create designs. This is a messy activity, and you may want to use smocks or aprons or have a bowl of water and towel handy for cleanup.

# PART 6
# Printing

# Sponge Printing

**MATERIALS NEEDED:**
White paper
Liquid tempera paint
Wet sponges
Shallow pans (pie tin or cake pan)

**PROCEDURE:**
- Place a small amount of liquid tempera paint in shallow pans.
- Give each child a sheet of paper.
- Be sure the sponges have been wrung out before starting.
- Allow the children to choose their sponges and paint colors.
- Let them dip their sponges into the paint and then press them onto the paper to create a print.
- Sponges cut out in various shapes are fun and interesting.

# Rubber Band Printing

**MATERIALS NEEDED:**
Matte board, cardboard, or other sturdy material
Powdered tempera paint
Liquid starch
Wood blocks
Rubber bands
Shallow pans (pie tin or cake pan)
Paper towels
Spoon

**PROCEDURE:**
- Mix powdered tempera paint and liquid starch into a fairly thick paint.
- Line the shallow pans with paper towels.
- Pour a very small amount of the paint onto the paper towels, and spread the mixture with a spoon.
- Give each child a piece of matte board, cardboard, or other base material.
- Give each child a wood block and a handful of rubber bands.
- Let the children wrap rubber bands around their blocks in any arrangement or design.
- Next, have them dip their blocks into the paint mixture and then press them onto their base material to create a print.

# Roller Printing

**MATERIALS NEEDED:**
White paper
Liquid tempera paint
Shallow pans (pie tin or cake pan)
Brayers
A variety of textured materials

**PROCEDURE:**
- Place a small amount of liquid tempera paint in shallow pans.
- Have a variety of materials with different texture available (such as sandpaper, velvet, mesh, or corrugated paper).
- Give each child a piece of paper.
- Have the children place their paper on the table and arrange some of the textured material underneath the paper.
- Have the children roll the brayer in the liquid tempera paint and then roll paint over their paper.
- Paint will pick up the texture of the material and a unique design will show.

# Leaf Prints

**MATERIALS NEEDED:**
Newsprint
Rice paper or plain white paper
Liquid tempera paint
Variety of leaves
Shallow pans (pie tin or cake pan)
Paintbrushes
Tongs

**PROCEDURE:**
- Place a small amount of liquid tempera paint in shallow pans.
- Have the children place a whole leaf on a piece of newsprint and then paint the leaf with a paintbrush.
- Once the children are done painting, have them pick their leaf up with their fingers or with tongs and place it painted side up on another clean sheet of newsprint.
- Next, have the children lay a clean sheet of rice paper (or any kind of thin white paper) over their leaf.
- Using a clean, dry paintbrush, have them brush over the top of the rice paper until it picks up the print of the leaf.

# Sandpaper Prints

**MATERIALS NEEDED:**
White paper
Sandpaper (medium grade)
Crayons
Electric iron (for adult use only)

**PROCEDURE:**
- Give each child a sheet of sandpaper.
- Ask them to draw heavily on the sandpaper using wax crayons.
- Place the sandpaper drawing side down onto a sheet of white paper.
- Iron the back of the sandpaper to transfer the design onto the white paper. An adult should complete this step.

# Crumpled Foil and Paper Prints

**MATERIALS NEEDED:**
Matte board, cardboard, or other sturdy material
Construction paper
Aluminum foil, newspaper, brown wrapping paper
Liquid tempera paint
Paintbrushes

**PROCEDURE:**
- Give each child a matte board, cardboard, or other base material and a piece of construction paper.
- Have the children paint with liquid tempera paint on their base material, covering the board entirely. (Paint should not be too thick.)
- Next, have them crumple a piece of foil, wrapping paper, or newspaper into a ball.
- Allow the children to roll their crumpled balls over their painted base material to create a print design.
- Next, have them roll the crumpled paper over the construction paper and see the new and interesting print.

Note: Be sure to use various kinds of paper to crumple. You may need to continue to add paint to the base material.

# Gadget Printing

**MATERIALS NEEDED:**
White paper
Liquid tempera paint
Shallow pans (pie tin or cake pan)
Gadgets or tools for printing (such as corks, spools, caps, potato mashers)
Newspaper

**PROCEDURE:**
- Place a small amount of paint in the shallow pans.
- Place on the table a variety of tools for printing: corks, spools, caps, potato mashers, whisks, rag mops for dishes, or anything with an interesting design.
- Give each child a sheet of paper. Have the children place their sheet on top of newspaper. The newspaper cushions the paper and gives a better print.
- Let the children press tools lightly into paint and then onto the paper.

# Glass Printing

**MATERIALS NEEDED:**
Sheets of Plexiglass or glass with protected edges
White paper
Liquid tempera paint
Water
Bowl
Paintbrushes
Sponges

**PROCEDURE:**
- Let the children take turns freely painting with liquid tempera on a piece of Plexiglass.
- When the children are finished painting, they may take a sheet of paper and press it onto the painted glass to create a print.
- When finished, each child should sponge off the glass for the next child to use. Make a fresh bowl of water and sponges available.

# Flower Printing

**MATERIALS NEEDED:**
White paper
Liquid tempera paint
Flowers (fresh)
Shallow pans (pie tin or cake pan)

**PROCEDURE:**
- Place a small amount of liquid tempera paint in shallow pans.
- Give each child a piece of paper.
- Have each child gently dip a flower into the paint.
- Have the children gently blot their flowers onto the paper to create a print.

# Spool Printing

**MATERIALS NEEDED:**
Matte board, cardboard, or other sturdy material
Liquid tempera paint
Spools of various sizes
Corks
Sponges
Cords or heavy yarn
Double-sided tape or rubber cement (for adult use only)
Shallow pans (pie tin or cake pan)
Paper towels
Spoon

**PROCEDURE:**
- Cut the corks and sponges into various shapes.
- Tape these shapes onto the body of the spools to create stamps. Cork, cord, or heavy yarn can be also be rubber-cemented onto the spools to create interesting stamps. An adult should complete this step.
- Line the shallow pans with paper towels.
- Pour a small amount of liquid tempera paint onto the paper towels and spread with a spoon.
- Give each child a matte board, cardboard, or other base material.
- Let the children roll the spools in the paint, and then roll them on their boards.
- When the children use spools having various designs, they can create their own combination effect.

# Tape Magic Print

**MATERIALS NEEDED:**
Matte board, cardboard, or other sturdy material
Chalk
Clear tape
Damp sponges

**PROCEDURE:**
- Give each child a piece of matte board, cardboard, or other base material.
- Have the children create a design on their board by placing clear tape in any pattern.
- Give each child a damp sponge.
- Have the children draw on their damp sponges with chalk, creating any design they choose.
- Next, allow them to dab their sponges onto their taped boards. The chalk will adhere to the places where there is no tape.
- Carefully remove the tape. Since the chalk adhered to the spaces outside of the tape designs, what you see is a negative space print.

# Lace Doily Prints

**MATERIALS NEEDED:**
Doilies in a variety of sizes and shapes
Colored construction paper
White liquid tempera paint
Bowls
Paintbrushes or sponges

**PROCEDURE:**
- Pour paint into bowls.
- Let the children choose a piece of colored construction paper.
- Have the children arrange a selection of doilies or doily pieces on their construction paper.
- Next, the children should dip a paintbrush or sponge into the white liquid tempera paint and lightly cover their doilies with the paint. Encourage the children not to use too much paint or the doilies will rip.
- After covering the doilies with paint, gently lift the doilies off the construction paper. This will give a reverse print on the paper.

# Plunger Prints

**MATERIALS NEEDED:**
Butcher paper
Liquid tempera paint
Cookie sheets
Plungers
Tape

**PROCEDURE:**
- Roll out a large piece of butcher paper onto the floor and tape it down.
- Place a small amount of liquid tempera paint on the cookie sheets and place these sheets around the butcher paper.
- Allow the children to dip plungers into the paint and then press the plungers onto the paper, thus creating a unique print.

# Shampoo Prints

**MATERIALS NEEDED:**
Matte board, cardboard, or other sturdy material
Shampoo
Water
Liquid watercolors
Trays
Mixing bowl
Paintbrushes
Electric mixer (for adult use only)

**PROCEDURE:**
- Pour about 2 teaspoons of shampoo into a mixing bowl.
- Add a small amount of water, and mix with the electric mixer until the consistency becomes like shaving cream. An adult should complete this step.
- Blend liquid watercolors into the mixture to create the desired color.
- Have the children use the mixture to paint directly on the tabletop or on a tray.
- Give each child a matte board, cardboard, or other base material.
- Have the children lightly press their boards on top of the shampoo mixture to create prints.

Variation: The shampoo mixture can also be used as fingerpaint.

# Shaving Cream Print

**MATERIALS NEEDED:**
Matte board, cardboard, or other sturdy material
Liquid tempera paint
Shaving cream

**PROCEDURE:**
- Squirt shaving cream directly onto the tabletop.
- Add color by putting a small amount of liquid tempera paint on the table.
- Let the children mix the color and shaving cream around with their hands, as in fingerpainting.
- If the children want to, they may make a print by taking a piece of matte board, cardboard, or paper and pressing it onto the tabletop design.

# Clay Block Printing

**MATERIALS NEEDED:**
White paper
Liquid tempera paint
Modeling clay
Spoons or craft sticks
Shallow pans (pie tin or cake pan)
Paper towels
Spoon
Wet sponges or rags

**PROCEDURE:**
- Have the children take a ball of modeling clay and thump it gently onto a flat surface so that one side of the ball is flat.
- Have them make a pattern or design in the flat side using a craft stick or spoon handle.
- Line the shallow tins with paper towel.
- Pour a small amount of liquid tempera onto the paper towels and spread with a spoon.
- Give each child a sheet of paper.
- Allow the children to press their clay designs into the paint and then press the clay onto the paper.
- Wipe the clay clean with a wet sponge or rag before reusing for printing.

# Splatter Printing

**MATERIALS NEEDED:**

White paper
Liquid tempera paint
Wooden frame with screening attached to top
Stencils or leaves
Bowls
Tray
Brushes (vegetable brushes, toothbrushes, scrub brushes)
Liquid starch (alternate)
Chalk (alternate)
Grater (alternate)

**PROCEDURE:**

- Cut out various stencils to create patterns for the children to use. Collect leaves if you would like to do leaf splatter. A variety of leaves with defined lines works best.
- Pour a small amount of liquid tempera paint into bowls. Do not use too many colors at a time; two colors produce a shadowy effect.
- Place one brush into each bowl.
- Place a tray with leaves or stencils on the table.
- Give each child a sheet of paper.
- Ask the children to take a selection of leaves or a few stencils and place them on their paper.
- Have the children take turns placing the wooden frame over their paper with their arrangement on it.
- Next, have them take a brush, dip it into the paint, and scrub back and forth across the screen. Have the children keep scrubbing until their white paper is completely covered with color.
- Lift the screen and see the lovely negative print.

Variation: Use colored chalk instead of paint. First, paint the white paper with liquid starch. Next, place the stencils on top of the starch-coated paper. Then grate chalk over the screen.

# Bubble Prints

**MATERIALS NEEDED:**
White paper
Liquid detergent
Water
Liquid watercolors
Bowls
Straws
Measuring cups and spoons

**MIXTURE (PER CHILD):**
2 tablespoons liquid detergent
1 cup water
10 drops liquid watercolors

Combine detergent, water, and liquid watercolors in bowl. Repeat for each color. This mixture works best if allowed to set overnight.

**PROCEDURE:**

- Give each child a bowl of liquid watercolors mixture and a straw.
- Give each child a sheet of white paper.
- Have the children put their straws into the bowl and blow out to make a large pile of bubbles.
- Next, have them take their sheet of white paper and gently pop the bubbles with the paper to create a bubble print.
- Children can trade different colors around the table and repeat the process so that each print has several colors.
- When the bowls are shared, be sure the children save their own straws to use again.

# Tin Can Roller

**MATERIALS NEEDED:**
White paper
Liquid tempera paint
Tin cans
Heavy cotton string
Rubber cement (for adult use only)
Shallow pans (pie tin or cake pans)
Paper towels
Spoon
Masking tape

**PROCEDURE:**

- Remove both ends of a tin can, ensuring that there are no sharp edges. Wash and dry the can, and then place masking tape over the ends to prevent possible cuts.
- Paint the outside of the can with rubber cement.
- Once covered in rubber cement, wrap cotton string around the can in various designs.
- Let the string can dry.
- Line the shallow tins with paper towels.
- Pour a small amount of liquid tempera paint onto the paper towels and spread it with a spoon.
- Give each child a sheet of paper.
- Have the children roll a can in the liquid tempera paint, and then roll the paint-covered can onto their paper, creating a design.

# Stamp Making

**MATERIALS NEEDED:**

Matte board, cardboard, or other sturdy material
Nondrying modeling clay
Liquid tempera paint
Plaster of paris
Water
Beads, bangles, corks, buttons, tiles, or other small objects
Paper or Styrofoam cup
Shallow pans (pie tins or cake pans)
Paper towels
Scissors
Spoons

**PROCEDURE:**

- Cut a paper or Styrofoam cup about halfway down from the top.
- Put clay into the bottom of the cup.
- Let the children push various printing materials—beads, buttons, bangles, tiles—into the clay.
- Mix plaster of paris and water and pour the mixture on top of the children's designs to the depth of 1 inch.
- Let the plaster harden, and then remove it from the cups. Each child will have a self-created stamp.

- Line the shallow pans with paper towels.
- Pour a small amount of liquid tempera onto the paper towels, and spread with a spoon.
- Give each child a piece of matte board, cardboard, or other base material.
- Have the children press their newly created stamps into the paint and then onto the base material to make a print.

# Plastic Clay Prints

**MATERIALS NEEDED:**

Matte board, cardboard, or other sturdy material

Heavy paper

Liquid tempera paint

Plasticine clay

Tile (small pieces), bangles, buttons, rings, or other small objects

Shallow pans (pie tin or cake pan)

Paper towels

Brayers

Paintbrushes

Blocks of wood or rolling pins

**PROCEDURE:**

- Give each child a matte board, cardboard, or other base material and some clay.
- Ask the children to warm the clay by working it with their hands.
- Have children pull small pieces of the clay off and press them in any pattern onto their boards.
- Once they have finished their clay designs, allow them to push small tiles, buttons, or bangles into the clay.
- Line the shallow pans with paper towels.
- Pour a small amount of liquid tempera onto the paper towels and spread with a spoon.
- Have the children paint their clay using paintbrushes and the liquid tempera or by rolling a brayer through the paint and then onto the clay.
- Once the clay pieces are colored, give each child a piece of heavy paper.
- Have the children press the paper onto their clay designs. Children can use a wood block to press down on the paper or can roll over it with a rolling pin.
- Finally, the children should lift their heavy paper off the clay design and see the negative print they have created.

# PART 7

# Just for Fun

# Placemats

**MATERIALS NEEDED:**

Clear contact paper

Flower petals, leaves, pine needles, tissue paper, or other small, flat objects

**PROCEDURE:**

- Place some place-mat-size rectangles of clear contact paper, sticky side up, on the table.
- Ask the children to arrange dried flower petals, tissue paper, spangles, or other small, flat objects on top of the contact paper.
- Once the children are finished, place the same size sheet of contact paper on top. Press together to form a placemat.

# Shoji Screens

**MATERIALS NEEDED:**

Waxed paper

Liquid starch

Grass, pine needles, flower petals, tissue paper, leaves, spangles, or other small, flat objects

Paintbrushes

Yarn

Hole punch

**PROCEDURE:**

- Tear off a piece of waxed paper about 12 inches long for each child.
- Have the children use paintbrushes to paint the entire waxed paper with liquid starch.
- Allow the children to choose materials from grass, pine needles, flower petals, tissue paper pieces, leaves, spangles, or other small, flat objects and arrange them on top of their starch-covered waxed paper.
- Give the children another piece of waxed paper the same length and help them place their second sheet over the top of their arrangement.
- Have them use their fingertips to gently press the waxed papers together. The papers will stick together as the starch dries.
- Punch a hole and put yarn through for hanging.
- Have the children hold their designs up to the light and watch it shine through.

# Body Trace

**MATERIALS NEEDED:**
Butcher paper
Felt-tip pens

**PROCEDURE:**
- Roll out a large piece of butcher paper onto the floor for each child.
- Have the children lie down on their paper.
- Trace around each child's body with a felt-tip pen.
- Ask the children to draw their own features, such as their eyes and nose and their clothes.

# Ornaments

**MATERIALS NEEDED:**
Felt-tip pens
White school glue
Trays
Fishing line
Hole punch
Scissors

**PROCEDURE:**

**Day 1**
- Give each child a tray.
- Let the children make designs on their trays using water-based felt-tip pens.
- Next, have the children pour enough white school glue onto their trays to cover their designs.
- Let the designs dry overnight.

**Day 2**
- Peel off the edges of the dried glue, and let their designs dry another day.

**Day 3**
- Peel the glue off of the trays completely.
- Have the children use scissors to cut designs out of the peeled dried glue.
- Punch a hole in the dried glue designs. Hang by fishing line.

# What Is That Smell?

**MATERIALS NEEDED:**
Flower petals, torn up
Water
Small containers
Bowls
Spoons
Masking tape

**PROCEDURE:**

- Have the children mix a few torn-up flower petals with a small amount of water in bowls.
- Stir the mixture until it looks yellow.
- Have the children pour the mixture into containers. It does not look appealing but smells very nice.
- Seal containers shut.

# Marbilizing

**MATERIALS NEEDED:**
Oil-based paint in several colors
Blown-out eggshells
Paper ornaments
Water
Bucket
Straw or heavy wire

**PROCEDURE:**

- Set out a bucket filled about halfway with water.
- Have the children select one or two colors of oil-based paint.
- Dribble several drops of each color into the water. It will not mix with the water.
- Allow the children to stir the water with a straw or heavy wire to swirl the colors around.
- Have each child select a paper ornament or eggshell.
- Attach long wires to the ornaments or eggshells so the children have something to hold on to. Have them dip their paper ornaments or eggshells into the water.
- Allow the children to swirl their ornaments around until they pick up the colors from the paint.
- Hang ornaments to dry overnight.

# Polka Dot and Tissue Design

**MATERIALS NEEDED:**
Dark-colored construction paper
Tissue paper
Bowls
White school glue thinned with water
Glue brushes
Hole punch

**PROCEDURE:**
- Give each child a sheet of construction paper.
- Have the children punch holes in the construction paper.
- Next, have them spread the watered-down glue thinly over a sheet of tissue paper.
- Have the children press their construction paper onto the glue on the tissue paper.
- Hold the papers up to the light or hang them in a window to see the light shine through their designs.

# Free-Form Ornaments

**MATERIALS NEEDED:**
Waxed paper
String cut to various lengths
White school glue thinned with water
Glitter
Bowls
Wet rag (for cleanup)

**PROCEDURE:**
- Give each child a piece of waxed paper.
- Have the children dip various pieces of string into bowls of watered-down glue. Have them run the string between their fingers to remove the excess glue. Have a wet rag ready to clean their hands.
- Next, allow the children to plop the string onto their waxed paper in any design.
- Allow them to sprinkle glitter on their string pieces.
- Let the decorated strings dry, and then peel them off the waxed paper.
- Once dry, the string designs can be hung as ornaments.

# Shimmer and Shine Wrapping Paper

**MATERIALS NEEDED:**
Heavy-duty aluminum foil
Tissue paper
White school glue thinned with water
Paintbrush
Confetti (optional)

**PROCEDURE:**
- Have the children tear or cut up tissue paper into small pieces.
- Give each child a piece of heavy-duty aluminum foil large enough to use as a piece of wrapping paper.
- Allow the children to arrange pieces of tissue on the foil in any pattern.
- Next, have them brush watered-down glue on the tissue scraps, completely covering them. Let the glue soak through.

Optional: Confetti pieces can be sprinkled onto the glue before it dries.

# Mixing Colors

**MATERIALS NEEDED:**
Liquid watercolors
Water
3 clear jars (Baby food jars work well.)
Egg cartons
Eyedroppers

**PROCEDURE:**
- Red, blue, and yellow are primary colors. When two of these colors are mixed together, they produce secondary colors: orange, green, purple. When mixed with clear water, they produce lighter shades of the same color.
- Have the children add red, blue, and yellow liquid watercolors to water in small clear jars with one color per jar.
- Give each child an egg carton with each cup filled with clear water.
- Allow the children to use eyedroppers to squirt the primary colors from the jars into their egg cartons.
- Have them combine different colors to see what happens. Talk about various colors.

# Sand Art

**MATERIALS NEEDED:**
Cornmeal
Powdered tempera paint
Bowls
Baby food jars
Small spoons
Cotton balls

**PROCEDURE:**

- Mix powdered tempera paint and cornmeal together in five separate bowls, one for each color.
- Give each child a baby food jar and a small spoon.
- Let the children spoon layers of the colored cornmeal mixture into their baby food jars until the jars are full. Do not shake or stir.
- Make sure the mixture is packed down in the jars, and then have the children put cotton balls on top. Screw the lids on tight.

Note: Don't let the children stir the mixture in their jars.

# Glossary of Art Material Terms

**Brayer:** A small roller, usually made of rubber. Found in art supply stores.

**Butcher paper:** Large white paper that comes on a roll and can be cut or torn off at the size you desire.

**Craft sticks:** Sticks from frozen juice or ice cream bars, or tongue depressors. Can also be bought at art supply stores.

**Driftwood:** Oddly shaped wood found at the beach.

**Eyedropper:** Used for medicinal purposes and can be bought at pharmacies.

**Liquid starch:** Blue starch in liquid form found at grocery stores.

**Liquid tempera:** Premixed water-based paint. Found in art and teacher supply stores.

**Liquid watercolor:** Preferred over food coloring because it's washable, it produces more vibrant colors, and it's easier to use.

**Matte board:** The material used to frame pictures. One side is a color and the other side is white. Found in frame stores and craft stores.

**Powdered tempera:** The dry form of water-based paint. Found in art and teacher supply stores.

**Watercolors:** Paints with a high water content. Found in art and teacher supply stores.

CPSIA information can be obtained
at www.ICGtesting.com
Printed in the USA
JSHW050515260623
43611JS00004B/6